Winners, Losers

Winners, Losers

THE 1976 TORY LEADERSHIP CONVENTION
Patrick Brown · Robert Chodos · Rae Murphy

James Lorimer & Company, Publishers
Toronto   1976

ISBN 0-88862-104-3 paper
          0-88862-105-1 cloth

Photographs by David Lloyd
Drawings by Aislin
Cover design by Emma Hess

5 4 3 2 1   76 77 78 79 80

A Last Post Book

James Lorimer & Company, Publishers
35 Britain Street
Toronto

Canadian Cataloguing in Publication Data

Brown, Patrick, 1947—
      Winners, losers

ISBN 0-88862-105-1 bd.
ISBN 0-88862-104-3 pa.

1. Progressive Conservative Party (Canada). National Convention, Ottawa, Ont., 1976.
I. Chodos, Robert, 1947—   II. Murphy, Rae, 1935—
III. Title.

JL197.P96B7   329.9'71   C76-017023-1

Contents

This is an outsider's view of the Progressive Conservative leadership race of 1975-76.

As outsiders we had many advantages. One was that we were not privy to the misinformation, baseless rumours, and outright lies that political insiders confide in each other. In fact, our only inside tip, one that Sinclair Stevens was going over to Clark, proved both right and wrong. It happened this way: one of us found a Stevens backer drinking it up in a Clark hospitality suite on Saturday evening. When pressed, the backer seemed to relish the prospect of Stevens as finance minister in a Joe Clark government. The information was relayed to our journalistic peers amid catcalls and jeers. As we now know, Sinc went to Joe. Our informant, however, went to Horner and, when his second choice dropped out, to the airport.

As outsiders we relied on press kit handouts; interviews with leadership candidates, which amounted to restatements of press kit handouts; interviews with various campaign officials, which amounted to restatements of press kit handouts; interviews with some prominent party people, which amounted to restatements of press kit handouts; and the newspapers, which amounted to restatements of press kit handouts. This recycling of information was made more efficient as the campaign really got rolling. The candidate would give his handout to the press, the reporter would write the article, the candidate would clip and xerox or multilith the article and hand it out again.

As outsiders we spoke to a number of delegates before, during and after the convention. We also went to a number of all-candidate and some-candidate and one-candidate meetings and read everything we could find on the events and issues surrounding the last Tory convention.

Not exhaustive research we suppose, but nevertheless exhausting.

So we didn't have the inside story of what was going on in Ottawa, but then neither did Brian Mulroney.

Prologue

Spoils to the Survivor

●

Quick Canadian Quiz: Who are **R. C. Quittenton, James Watson, Joe Clark, Winnett Boyd, Joseph Zappia** and **John Franklin?**

●

Quiz answer: They're all candidates to succeed **Robert Stanfield** as leader of the federal Progressive Conservative Party.

●

— Toronto *Star*, December 1975

There is a fundamental law of trench warfare, developed in the crucible of battle, that goes like this: "It is not enough to keep your head down when other people are shooting at you, you must have your head down before they take aim." Knowledge of it has helped thousands of soldiers return safely from what would otherwise have been extremely hazardous locations.

It also helps explain why Charles Joseph Clark emerged from the Conservative convention as leader of the party, while Brian Mulroney had to hustle back to his law practice in Montreal.

Mulroney wowed the press, but his posing and preening put him in range. He was up front, and by convention time there was no army behind him — just a brick wall.

Meanwhile, Joe Clark was in the trench, making friends and telling Tories the things they wanted to hear. But nobody seemed to notice. As it turned out, Clark was lucky to be sandbagged by the press. He was lucky that, for example, the Toronto Star, which had between twenty-five and thirty reporters covering every piece of trivia in Ottawa, couldn't find one reporter to cover a Toronto press conference in late January to hear Clark announce the support of four Alberta cabinet ministers, and thus the implied good wishes of the Man Himself in Edmonton.

Clark was lucky—really lucky—that nobody seemed to notice that the only candidate that Dalton Camp had nice things to say

about right through the campaign was Joe Clark. Camp was supporting Mulroney, everyone knew that, and it was enough to put
Mulroney's chin in the range of another column of the Diefenbaker Armoured Division.

Clark was lucky enough that nobody bothered to research the
fact that he was almost a charter member of the Get Diefenbaker
Club—he worked for Davie Fulton, the first declared anti-Die-
fenbaker leadership candidate, in '67—and he was Robert Stanfield's executive assistant, in which capacity he must have handled a lot of the messages between Stanfield and Camp.

Clark, of course, was astute enough not to stress such things.
His stock answer about Diefenbaker was the Chief brought him
into politics, inspired him in the fifties with The Vision. Clark's
little group of Western musicians, which was by a country mile
the best at the convention, sang "Dief Will Be The Chief Again"
after almost every rendition of "Old Joe Clark".

The relevant data on Clark's background, however, is contained in two lines of his official biography:

Special Assistant to the Honourable Davie Fulton, 1967.

Executive Assistant to the Honourable Robert L. Stanfield,
1967-70.

Somebody should have noticed their significance. But no one
was paying attention.

Above all, Clark was lucky that the media chose Mulroney as
their very own candidate: He was lucky that Ingrid Saumart in
La Presse chose Mulroney to be "dynamic, bilingual and seduc-
tive." Lucky also that in Calgary the *Herald* said Mulroney has
"that carved in granite, made in heaven look that political publi-
cists love to sell in public."

Lucky that it was Mulroney the Edmonton *Journal* was
describing when it printed "The eyes are Paul Newman blue, his
hair has the swoop of the Robert Redford style, and voice the
resonance of a Lorne Greene school of broadcasting. The jaw is
by Gibraltar." And when the real heavy hitter, Richard Gwyn,
chose Mulroney to be the star of his piece about how the media
were going to choose the next leader, Clark was home free. The
press, as anyone who was mugged in the Château Laurier or
kicked in the shins by little old ladies with cleats on their toes for
wearing a media pass knows, is not liked by Conservatives. But
that doesn't mean they don't read it, watch it and even listen to
it.

At the same time, all the attention paid to Mulroney established that the candidacy of a young man with little or no parliamentary experience was legitimate and could be sold to a broad

spectrum of the party. As the convention approached Clark was being described as the thinking man's Brian Mulroney — but not loudly enough to do him much damage.

It was a combination of astuteness and luck that won it all for Joe Clark on that weekend in Ottawa. This, of course, is what this book chronicles. But let it be said at the outset that this Tory convention was not a popularity contest, but an unpopularity contest. Like a war. The spoils go not to the victor, but to the survivor. Neither friend nor foe noticed Joe Clark until there was no time to take aim.

Winners & Losers

> **Mr. Sinclair Stevens (York-Simcoe):** Mr. Speaker, in the absence of the Minister of Finance I will put my question to the Prime Minister.
> **An Hon. Member:** Another Red Tory.
> **Some Hon. Members:** Oh, oh.
> — House of Commons Debates, February 24, 1976

Since under most conditions hotel lobbies are not major producers of revenue, not much floor space is wasted on them by modern hotel architects. Ottawa's Skyline is a modern hotel, and its small lobby was crowded with Tory conventioneers throughout. Compounding the overcrowding, the hotel rented every available bit of space to the candidates for information booths. They also rented every foot of unavailable space for posters—the New China News Agency correspondent covering the event, remembering the large character poster campaign during the Cultural Revolution, must have felt quite at home.

Since an information booth isn't an information booth without a crowd, every candidate organized a cluster of supporters to mill about constantly waving signs and handing out invitations to Hoedowns, Speakeasys, Hospitality Suites, Eat Grits Breakfasts, Maritimes Luncheons and other events, including a luncheon with such regional delicacies as Ontario boiled eggs and Saskatchewan rolls.

An information booth also isn't an information booth without noise, and so bands of all shapes, sizes and descriptions spotted themselves about the place.

On Friday, February 20, the normal confusion in the lobby of the Skyline was compounded by the series of policy sessions that were conducted throughout the day in the various meeting rooms. The hotel was a surging, seething mass of Tory humanity moving good-naturedly but purposefully from one hall to the other. The delegates were on their appointed rounds to hear and question the various leadership candidates. And nothing would divert them. Even the odd provocative shout, such as "Isn't that John Turner over there near Mulroney's booth?" (it was), caused the shoals of delegates to shift course only briefly.

It was here, pinned against a wall, eating a Nowlan apple, that one of us was accosted by a university student bearing a clip-board and questionnaire. She was looking for delegates, and a mere apple-munching observer of the passing parade was something she was told not to waste time upon.

However, we did learn that the questionnaire sought to determine whether there was "an ideological split between left and right in the Conservative Party."

The answer, we found out in a subsequent release by Professor George Perlin of Queen's University, was that no split existed, that, indeed, the whole thing was a will o'the wisp being chased by the media.

The Toronto *Sun* reported on Tuesday, February 24:

> The survey indicates that 60 per cent of the delegates viewed themselves as reformers, progressives, liberals or so-called Red Tories—the left side of the party. Only seven per cent felt there was an irreconcilable left-right split.
>
> Mr. Perlin said the vast majority of delegates surveyed felt that there was no relevance in a conflict between Dalton Camp, former national president of the party, and John Diefenbaker.
>
> He said 85 per cent of the delegates indicated they would not be influenced by the opinions of Mr. Camp or Mr. Diefenbaker in their selection of a new leader.
>
> Mr. Perlin said that Sinclair Stevens' alliance with the Joe Clark camp during the convention was a clear demonstration that a formidable left-right split does not exist.
>
> Mr. Stevens, who was described as a right-wing extremist candidate, was able to go over to the Red Tory camp because such extreme divisions do not exist, he said.
>
> When Paul Hellyer took on an extremist posture in his speech to the convention, he was playing on a stereotype which he thought meant something to the delegates.

Dr. Perlin's survey poses a number of problems — chief among which are the questions asked.

First of all any Tory with even an elementary regard for life and limb would sooner have walked into the Civic Centre arm in arm with Fidel Castro and Pierre Trudeau than with Dalton Camp. This of course didn't stop the majority of the delegates from voting for a leader of the party in the Camp mould. This presumably would represent the 60 per cent of the delegates who considered themselves to be "reformers, progressives, liberals or so-called Red Tories."

Second, if John Diefenbaker could not influence delegates, what was the exercise on the first night of the convention all about?

And third, there could be several reasons why Sinclair Stevens went to Clark instead of Hellyer:

(a) The bulk of his delegation was going to Clark anyhow.

(b) He has a few scores to settle with Jack Horner over the star-crossed Bank of Western Canada.

(c) Not many people tried to board the Hindenburg for the return trip.

There is indeed a split in the Tory party. The split is evident not only in the result of the final ballot, but in the voting pattern that emerged from the first ballot on. The problem is to define its context.

This division explains why the delegates worked ·so hard at this convention, why the candidates were questioned so closely during the months before the convention and at the convention itself, and above all, why the convention could not be brokered and why it was perhaps the closest thing to a genuine display of intraparty democracy that any Canadian political party has ever staged.

Because the party represents such a broad and diverse section of Canada with more conflicting than common interests, and because all the major candidates were unique in the programs they espoused it is difficult, and perhaps irresponsible to attempt to label anyone in the Progressive Conservative party of 1976 as left or right.

Even in these days of situational ethics, situational politics and situational labels, in which we speak with a straight face and serious mien about the left wing of the Spanish Falange and the right wing of the Chinese Politburo, to call Joe Clark's supporters "a bunch of Reds", as one of Jack Horner's brothers is reported to have done, is really stretching it somewhat.

There is perhaps slightly more validity in personifying the struggle around names: Stanfield vs. Diefenbaker. But that only confuses things more. The conventional wisdom in 1967 was that the getting of Diefenbaker by Camp and Stanfield was a move to the right. How and why did things get reversed?

The only way even to approach the context of the split in the

Tory party is, borrowing a phrase from Kurt Vonnegut, to call it a split between the winners and the losers.

The Tory party, having been out of office federally for so long, is a party of losers. Its mass appeal now and perhaps its greatest prospect for the future is that with the euphoria of the sixties over many people feel they are, and feel safer with, losers.

But even in a party of losers, there is such a thing as carrying matters too far.

The problem for the Tories is to convert this undefined and unorganized dissatisfaction into enough energy to propel them into government. One half of the party was working on this problem and the other half was working on trying to settle old scores. That is one reason why the speeches of John Diefenbaker and Robert Stanfield, successive leaders who spoke on successive evenings before the same crowd in the same language, had absolutely no common thread.

There are some people in the party, whom we might call 'governmentalists' or at least would-be winners, who realize, all demagogy and political sight-reading aside, that government is here to stay, and that as society becomes more complex government will also. There are others, the 'oppositionalists' or bedrock losers, who are looking for a bio-degradable government. The code words for the latter are Free Enterprise. Ironically, while Free Enterprise was becoming the rallying cry in the boardrooms of Canada's protected monopolies at the turn of the year, the 'oppositionalists' were losing their struggle to regain control of the Conservative party.

Governments when they are elected in Canada face the same exigencies and react to them in roughly the same manner whatever their political faith. There is scant difference on, say, wage and price controls between NDP, Tory, Liberal and even Social Credit governments in Canada. The dreaded bureaucracy, with its 'freedom-restricting' chains of regulation and red tape, has grown equally in Liberal Ottawa, Tory Toronto and Socialist Winnipeg. We can have fun and games with "bringing government back to the people," but sooner or later serious politicians organize to bring a serious party back to serious business.

It is no coincidence that very few Tory provincial cabinet ministers or important municipal politicians were seen holding hands with Horner, Hellyer, Nowlan or Wagner.

No one understands these things better than William Davis, and that is why his speech decrying the evils of government spending was so unintentionally funny (those are the only kind of funny speeches he can make). If it hadn't been for his constant references to Trudeau and the Liberals one would have thought he was lacing into his own government.

Not only that, but William Davis also sends his cabinet ministers on junkets to China and Cuba, presumably to deal with the same dastardly Commies whom his fellow Tories spent so much time denouncing at the convention and who are supposed to have Trudeau and his ministers in their pockets.

It is also in terms of a flexible division between winners and losers that the chronology of the leadership campaign can best be understood. The campaign divided itself roughly into three phases: an opening game, in which the participants tried to stake out positions while still keeping their options open, a middle game, in which the board became crowded but patterns began to emerge, and an end game, in which only a few pieces were left standing and the final shakedown occurred.

It happened more or less like this:

July-September

——Losers lay plans to get Stanfield out of the way. Château Cabinet comes out of the shadows. Winners decide that if Stanfield cannot stay as leader they will move in on party machinery to make sure they run the convention.

——Stanfield resigns, sends out feelers for appeals begging him to stay on, but only Peter Reilly and Dalton Camp respond.

——Most potential candidates are hiding in the weeds. Flora MacDonald has Toronto lawyer Eddie Goodman sending letters for funds, but has not yet declared. Only Heward Grafftey is officially in the race. "We must stop Trudeau's socialism," says Grafftey. Nobody is listening. Toronto *Star* headline says "One running — but Tory race is crowded."

——Jockeying for delegates begins in Quebec. Claude Wagner not declared, but his forces take early lead. Rumours of coming credentials fight at convention.

——John Robarts, Darcy McKeough and Allan Lawrence campaigns appear and quickly disappear.

——Ontario Tory government reduced to minority. Big Blue Machine sent back to shop for repairs, will not be ready for convention.

——Toronto's Mayor David Crombie agonizes over decision to run. Tories put him out of his agony.

October-November

——Rumours abound but Peter Lougheed is nowhere in sight.

——Overtures are made to John Turner, but ex-finance minister is mum.

——First volume of John Diefenbaker's memoirs appears. Dief is appointed Living Legend.

——Young, "with-it" Montreal lawyer appears uninvited at Dief's 80th birthday party. The Mulroney balloon drifts upward and is watched through field-glasses in both bunkers.

——Mulroney is given 10-1 chance by Toronto *Star.* So is Charles Clark (sic).

——Serious engagements begin in Quebec. Leaks about Wagner trust fund beginning to trickle into newspapers, are confirmed by Wagner.

——Sniper fire between Dalton Camp and Château Cabinet.

December

——Outlaw candidacy of Leonard Jones provides momentary diversion.

——All candidates try to divide the turf. Sinclair Stevens claims to be sitting in the centre while leaning to the right —will later say he looks cuddly sitting on an angle.

——Victory of Sterling Lyon over Sidney Spivak at Manitoba provincial leadership convention is interpreted as triumph for the right wing of the party.

——Losers looking for standard-bearer. Paul Hellyer seems likely for the job but delays declaration.

——Serious search begins for Least Hated Tory.

——Trudeau muses about New Society. Business community and Tories flummoxed.

January

——Grafftey warns Tories not to let Trudeau drive them too far to right. Warning not heeded, especially by Grafftey.

——Jones disqualified. Camp and Diefenbaker both take issue with decision but others breathe sigh of relief.

——Tories begin to sense that Trudeau is vulnerable and the leadership looks more attractive. Delegates begin to eliminate undesirables but since almost everybody seems undesirable to somebody no consensus emerges.

——Vancouver *Sun* columnist Allan Fotheringham writes: "There are, at the moment, five serious candidates left in the stumbling race toward the Tory leadership. They are Claude Wagner, Brian Mulroney, Flora MacDonald, Sinclair Stevens and Paul Hellyer."

February

——Peter Regenstreif poll declares Wagner, Mulroney front-runners. Aim taken on Mulroney balloon from all sides.

——Battle that was begun in Toronto's Maple Leaf Gardens in 1967 is rejoined in Ottawa's Civic Centre.

——The universe unfolds, if not as it should, at least as it usually does.

The dangers of trying to fit the division in the Tory party into too rigid an ideological cast were perhaps best illustrated by the unlikely alliance that developed between Sinc Stevens and Joe Clark. While they may not agree on matters of political philosophy, their ambitions coincided at a crucial point. Neither has exactly reached his goal yet, but both are a step further along the road.

We had had little impression of Stevens before entering his office in the Centre Block for an interview in November. We knew that he was contesting the leadership on a right-wing platform and vaguely remembered his name from a row over the stillborn Bank of Western Canada some years back, a controversy that, like so many others, seemed to have faded with time.

Stevens himself had only a little time for us and foisted us onto Don Blenkarn, a self-proclaimed country lawyer from Mississauga and former MP who was managing his leadership campaign. It was a disquieting encounter. The inspiration for the campaign Blenkarn wanted to run seemed to be Barry Goldwater's doomed bid for the American presidency in 1964. He talked about conservative philosophy and about giving the voters a real alternative. "If we keep on the route we're going," said Blenkarn, "we won't be a free nation."

The next morning we were to talk to another of the leadership candidates. Our impressions of Joe Clark were equally sketchy. At the opening of Parliament in 1973, just after his initial election to the House, he had struck up a conversation with one of us at an Ottawa reception. The conversation revolved around railways and the preservation of small communities, on which he was informed and interesting. At the height of the anti-bilingualism, anti-welfare backlash that had resulted in a near-victory for the Conservatives, it was a bit refreshing to come across a Tory whose views seemed reasonable and thought-out. Especially one from Alberta. The name, Joe Clark, forgettable as it was, stuck somewhere in the back of the mind.

The impression he had created then was strongly reinforced now. With all the other candidates, he shared a distaste for government spending. But he recognized that the problems the government was spending money in an attempt to solve were generally real ones, and that if federal programs were abandoned other initiatives would have to be taken to deal with them. He argued that such action was often better undertaken at the local level, and suggested that the federal government should empower the provinces to make more money available to local governments for community programs. His enthusiasm for community action rivalled that of a 1960s New Leftist. He proposed that Ottawa, instead of having universal programs that were insufficient in some parts of the country and unnecessary in others, should have specific programs to deal with specific situations. And he conceded that if all this were done it might cost more than the government was currently spending, initially at least, but the important thing was that the money would be more effectively applied.

We felt that in these back-to-back interviews we had seen the poles of the party. Impressive as Clark was, he did not seem to have a chance of winning. The mood of the party appeared to be, if anything, closer to Stevens, and anyway in the end the Conservatives would probably reject both poles and choose someone who could emerge as a compromise candidate, someone who was able to be all things to all people. Brian Mulroney, for instance.

In mid-October, three weeks before we had met Clark and Stevens, Mulroney had outlined in an interview the scenario of a successful campaign for the leadership. First of all, the delegates would vote for someone who looked like a winner; the Tories were tired of being in opposition and wanted a Prime Minister. Second, the successful candidate had to appeal to both major factions of the party. Third, he had to have a certain credibility in Quebec. Fourth, he shouldn't be too specific on policy. Specific policy proposals had been the party's downfall in the past; the Liberals won the 1974 election by forcing the Tories to defend their wage and price controls proposal rather than having to defend their own record. Brian Mulroney wouldn't make the same mistake.

And finally, Mulroney would turn his most glaring liability, his lack of electoral experience and unfamiliarity to the public at large, into an asset. The candidates were a sufficiently motley group that whoever won would, to some degree, be coming out of the blue. Mulroney was no more unknown in Edmonton than John Fraser or Sinclair Stevens was in Montreal. Besides, much of what was known about the better-known candidates would hurt rather than help them.

It was, on the whole, a shrewd assessment of the situation. The only problem was that, in the end, Mulroney, the endlessly flexible man, didn't run the campaign he outlined. Joe Clark, the

ideologue, did. And Sinc Stevens, the diametrically opposed ideologue, sealed his victory for him.

"Brian's candidacy will inflate," said Clark in November,
"and then deflate." Even he must have been surprised at the size
of the inflation and the speed of the deflation.

Paul Hellyer

Wednesday

UNITY NOW, AND VICTORY NEXT,
L'UNITE VERS LE POUVOIR.
MULRONEY! MULRONEY! MULRONEY!

The Hoopla Group is jazzing it up at ten o'clock Wednesday morning in Ottawa Station. Fresh from the Ontario Liberal leadership convention, the group is a six-man ensemble that does convention gigs. They were the musical muscle behind Stanfield in '67. Joining in on the chorus are about a hundred placard-waving supporters, who have been rounded up with some difficulty.

They're there to meet The Candidate, who comes in on the 10:15 from Montreal, accompanied by his tantalizingly-pregnant wife Mila and what appears to be a working majority of the Quebec Bar Association. Brian Mulroney says A Few Words to the crowd.

The welcomers pile into two buses, heading for the Skyline Hotel. The Mulroney party climbs into cars, to drive around for a while, making sure that the welcomers have time to get to the Skyline first to set up another ecstatic welcome. They do.

The scene in the lobby is an assault on the senses. The Mulroney song is deafening, the Mulroney uniforms and placards dazzling. The Candidate and his aides struggle through the crowd, beaming, hand-shaking and saying a few words, making their way to the elevator. As the doors close, shutting out the pandemonium, the smiles are turned off and the Mulroney machine rides up some twenty floors in total silence. When they're out of the public eye, candidates have a blank look that people who've been in the trenches call the thousand-yard stare. By convention time they're shell-shocked, and running on automatic pilot.

In his suite, Mulroney changes his shirt, which he does five times a day (the significance of this will be explored later), and then goes back down to the lobby for yet a third thunderous welcome, at the special request of CTV, which had forgotten to put film in its camera for the first two.

Whaddya Hear?

Nobody is at the Ottawa station to welcome the Last Post Outasight Team when it arrives later in the day.

Along with some 1400 other media types we are processed in the Assembly Hall of the Civic Centre. It is a fair-sized room with tables of typewriters and telephones, a couple of TV sets, a teletype machine, a beer bar, a free coffee urn and a table where cheese and crackers and sandwiches are for sale. The room is staffed by some of the dimmer lights in the Tory firmament. Things are moving slowly — accreditations are misplaced, the camera breaks down for a while and our mug-shots are delayed — but in its own haphazard way the system seems to be functioning reasonably smoothly.

A brief tour of the arena — a mass of posters, lights, cameras and cables. All available space is plastered with posters, with Mulroney and Wagner clearly ahead in the poster-plastering stakes. Someone tells us that Mulroney hired a firm of professional poster-plasterers to do his, while the rest were put up by zealous volunteers. In one corner we notice a tiny yellow sign on a door, presumably the last remnant of some previous convention:

CYRIL MORGAN
FOR SECOND VICE PRESIDENT

It is refreshing to come across a man of such modest ambitions.

Everything is being tested out. High in the galleries spotters with field glasses and walkie-talkies are issuing orders to people on the floor and in various sections — a dry run for Sunday. We pace off the arena, find where all the candidates will be seated, count the telephones in every section and do other useless reconnaissance.

As a status symbol a walkie-talkie is all right, but it doesn't hold a candle to a bellboy. A little box tucked in the inside jacket pocket that beeps and pings when the wearer is wanted not only indicates a higher state of importance than a walkie-talkie, but also has the advantage that anyone who rates being wired up to one can carry it everywhere instead of just on the floor of the convention.

The prestige attached to the bellboy becomes clear at a reception for the media hosted by the executive of the party at the National Press Club. One of us approaches a man standing in the middle of the throng with credentials on his chest like a line of battle ribbons: "You a delegate?" "I'm a Member of Parliament," he replies, and shows us the bellboy that marks him as a man of substance. He distils the essence of the convention into one sentence: "Everybody in the caucus will jump up and salute whoever comes into next week's meeting wearing lederhosen."

This explanation seems too simple, and we move through the crowd trying to engage in conversation and overhear others. There is no lack of stories and rumours, but mostly everyone is working hard at being bored with it all. "Jesus," one reporter says, "I just spent a week with Hellyer in Newfoundland and was it ever scary."

"Who, Hellyer?"

"No, Newfoundland."

We also bump into the UPI correspondent, who asks us, "Whaddya hear?"

We say we don't hear much, and ask what he hears. He says he hears that a deal has been struck between Wagner and Hellyer, to the effect that Wagner is going to deliver his people to Hellyer on the second ballot. He has just been explaining the inevitability of such an outcome to the Canadian people on CBC radio's *As It Happens.*

"Whaddya hear?" is the universal opening line among the press, and what is heard, and recounted in confidential tones, is generally as reliable as UPI's hot tip.

Occasionally a candidate enters the room and cameras pop. The crowd jostles as the candidates move to press the flesh.

Brian Mulroney sweeps in followed by his entourage. "How have things been going since we last had lunch?" someone asks him. Mulroney squints to read the name on the lapel. "Just great," he says, and moves on.

Joe Clark is standing in a corner talking to whoever comes by.

Heward Grafftey appears at the door and no one seems to be paying any attention to him. One of us asks him, "Who are your delegates going to go to if you're eliminated?" "My delegates are pretty independent-minded," he says. "They have to be to support me."

Finally the bar closes and the gathering breaks up. As people are fishing for their coats and squeezing into the elevator, a tall, distinguished-looking man arrives and is halfway to the centre of the room before he realizes to his chagrin that he is a little late.

It is our first sign that the Paul Hellyer campaign is in deep trouble.

Paul Hellyer was a senior cabinet minister, then a Liberal backbencher, then an Action Canada backbencher, then a Tory backbencher, then a former Tory backbencher and a columnist for the Toronto *Sun*. It wasn't exactly a steady uphill course.

Yet one segment of the Conservative party got it into its collective head that Hellyer could be the instrument through which the party could be recaptured and set back onto its true course. That it didn't happen had much to do with the candidate himself, but also much to do with the people who backed him and the nature of their crusade.

Hellyer was the last of the major contenders to enter, and made much of the support he was able to round up from some twenty-five Conservative MPs. These MPs fell into three broad categories. First there were some of the more prominent Diefenbaker loyalists, such as Sean O'Sullivan, the 23-year-old overachiever from Hamilton-Wentworth, and Jake Epp from Manitoba, who declared his own candidacy early in the campaign to act as a stalking horse for Hellyer. Then there were some eastern-Ontario anti-bilingualism hardliners, such as Tom Cossitt of Leeds and Doug Alkenbrack of Frontenac-Lennox and Addington. And finally there was a group described by one reporter covering the Hellyer campaign as "members who have been in the House for years and never made a speech, and seeing them in the campaign you realized why. Most of them can't have IQs above 90." The presence of Diefenbaker friend and admirer Dr. Jimmy Johnston in its Ottawa office gave the Hellyer campaign a distinctive stamp—this was to be the campaign to get the guys who got the guys last time.

The revivalist fervour with which Hellyer holds his opinions masks the fact that they are, with few exceptions, fairly commonplace ones. His 1971 book *Agenda: a Plan for Action*, intended as a manifesto for the Action Canada movement he was unsuccessfully trying to get off the ground, was largely a turgid restatement of conventional liberal philosophy and simplistic neo-capitalist economics, in many ways not unlike Pierre Trudeau's recent ramblings.

(It is reported that as Hellyer was struggling with the outline for his book, he confided to a friend that he envisaged three sections: one in which he summarized Western thought, one in which he discussed the problems as he saw them, and one in which he presented his solutions. The friend said that the last two sections sounded fine, but that Western thought business, well, some pretty heavy hitters had tackled it and it was tricky stuff. "I know," said Paul. "I've been reading up on it for three months.")

The book contained only one policy proposal that was in any way new or startling.

"Huge corporations and unions," wrote Hellyer, "cannot and probably should not be dissolved. At the same time, however, their influence on prices and incomes is often detrimental to the public interest. It is necessary, therefore, to implement wage and price guidelines. Although I expect business and labour would co-operate in development of an improved system, because they are law-abiding citizens for the most part, I am not so naive to think they will do it voluntarily . . . Consequently, the only workable solution involves making the price and wages guidelines mandatory."

This was two years before the idea of controls was adopted by Jim Gillies, three years before it was adopted by Robert Stanfield, and four years before it was adopted by Pierre Trudeau. During the campaign, after controls had become a Liberal measure and hence opposed by the Tories, he reiterated his espousal of them and criticized the government's program only in detail. Unlike Trudeau or Stanfield, he has also said that the controls should in principle be permanent.

None of this seemed to faze his free-enterprise followers, for whom Paul was going to restore the fundamental freedoms that were being taken away by That Man at 24 Sussex. If you asked Hellyer supporters where their candidate stood on permanent controls, they would generally tell you that he was against them. Hellyer supporters weren't the sort who read books.

On other issues Hellyer, despite his reputation for single-mindedness, has not been noticeably more consistent than most other politicians. In 1969, he resigned from the cabinet because his housing program was rejected by Trudeau, who said it would violate provincial jurisdiction. Seven years later, in a campaign interview with Le Devoir, he came out strongly in favour of decentralization and turning more power over to the provinces. "I'm thinking," he said, "particularly of certain aspects of the activity of the Central Mortgage and Housing Corporation. In the matter of urban redevelopment, Ottawa has no business telling Toronto, Montreal, Quebec City or Halifax how to do it. Certain CMHC norms make no sense when they are uniform on a national scale."

Hellyer is perhaps most noticeably to the right of the political mainstream in his attitude toward trade unions, but even there getting tough with the unions is a stance that has been adopted recently by everybody from Bryce Mackasey to Dave Barrett (with varying results). Hellyer however goes a little bit farther. When pressed, he admits that it may be impossible to control business, which means that his controls would in effect apply primarily to the unions. He also favours making unions subject to anti-combines legislation, a backward leap of more than sixty years in labour law.

Ten days before the convention, Hellyer outlined to Toronto *Star* reporter Michael Benedict what he had learned from his defeat in the Liberal leadership contest of 1968.

"At the '68 convention," wrote Benedict, "the bottom fell out of the campaign the night before the balloting. Never a stirring platform performer, Hellyer read word-for-word a dry speech which he says lost him about 150 votes.

" 'I gave a terrible speech. It would have been better if I hadn't said anything at all,' he says now.

"This time around, Hellyer doesn't plan to make the same mistake. He'll make a speech, but it will be off the cuff, he says."

"They serving booze down in Gillies' room?" asks our host in one of Claude Wagner's suites.

"Yes, they sure are," we answer, with perhaps unwarranted enthusiasm since we don't even know where Gillies' suite is.

He passes us a plate of doughnuts that look as if they were stale when they were baked. His face clouds momentarily and he mutters something under his breath.

The suite is almost deserted. We drink coffee and chat with a couple from Winnipeg.

Mulroney's gang, we are told, moved into Manitoba and put Sterling Lyon into Sidney Spivak's job as leader. It was a dirty job: "We think there was a bit of anti-Semitism connected with it." Anyway, the true blue Manitoba group is behind Wagner 100 per cent. The other gang can have their Mulroney.

Aside from that rather unexpected revelation there isn't much happening. We swallow our coffee and take leave.

The host is talking with a couple of delegates who have paused in the doorway. He is jabbing his finger at a picture of Wagner taped against the open door. "This man here, has built the party in Quebec. We had nothing. Now there's organization everywhere."

"Just a wonderful man . . . wonderful," says the lady by the coffee urn. "Come in for a moment for some coffee." "Yeah, have some coffee . . . sorry we can't offer you anything stronger but there's no booze here yet."

He emphasizes the "yet" and we vow to check the suite out again. One purpose of our investigations will be to find out where and when the first chinks in the embargo on free booze occur.

We make our way to the lobby of the Château Laurier, which is festooned with posters and signs, hats and scarves. Mulroney's campaign appears to dominate the lobby. He has also rented the adjacent salon and there is coffee, sandwiches, a cash bar and a giant television screen which is currently running a video-tape of The Man Himself.

Fleshing out the crowd are legions of attractive Mulroney workers—most we talked to claim to be volunteers, but the rumour persists that most were hired. Many of them wear the distinctive Mulroney costume—shirts for the men and skirts for the women with a motif of the now familiar blue and white hexagon with Brian Mulroney's face beaming from the middle. "We all paid for these skirts ourselves," says one well manicured, coiffured and facialed lady. She does look as if she can afford her own clothes.

Red, white and blue are the dominant colours of the convention, largely because of the omnipresence of the Mulroney shirts and skirts. Toronto *Sun* editor Peter Worthington will draw on his experiences in Africa to note that the Mulroney costume harkened to Zaire and Uganda where the natives have taken to wearing clothes with their leaders' faces as part of the pattern. Worthington implies that he will, on another occasion, draw some more important parallels between Patrice Lumumba and Brian Mulroney. A more widely noted parallel is the similarity between the Mulroney hexagon and the Trudeau symbol at the Liberal leadership convention of 1968.

Joe Clark's colours aren't as ubiquitous as Mulroney's, but he does get the corner on bright yellow and black. Flora MacDonald tries for an off-brown and off-grey — we are told more than once that it is terra cotta.

Hellyer, Wagner and Horner supporters wear hats and don't seem to worry about any colour combinations. The Wagner men seem to favour basic double-breasted pin-stripes and shades. Mulroney, Clark and MacDonald don't bother with hats and concentrate on scarves.

Automobile logos also seem to be highly favoured. Hellyer's logo is an adaptation of Chevrolet's, while Sinclair Stevens' stylized "S" looks remarkably like that of the old Studebaker. And Joe Clark has the typeface and colour of Hertz Rent-a-Car.

Meanwhile, the action is clearly in Joe Clark's room.

The place is jumping, the cash bar is pushing the beer and liquor and we remember just how thirsty we are. One of us is dispatched down to the lobby for the necessary booze tickets.

By now the lobby is really crowded. It is a friendly, excited and happy crowd, who seem to enjoy the attention they are being given by the various campaign workers—leaflets, brochures, buttons and stickers are pushed freely around and none seems to be turned aside.

In the crowded elevator returning to the Clark hospitality suite we receive our first inkling of what is eventually to become a dominant mood of the convention. Joe Clark, although not exactly well known, is not as unknown as we have been led to believe. Very few delegates have come to Ottawa to vote for him, but unlike Mulroney, almost nobody has come to vote against him.

When the elevator doors finally open on the third floor, an elderly delegate with whom we have been talking on the way up decides to visit Clark's rooms. Just as we leave the elevator we catch the tail end of a procession of yellow-scarved banjo pluckers and assorted singers and signbearers heading down the corridor.

As we get in step, the elderly man says, "I wonder which one of those kids is Joe."

In fact, however, Clark is in the centre of the room, chatting with the throng of people around him and waiting for the spontaneous musical ensemble to reach him. The room is crowded but we push in with the musicians, at least as far as the fringes of the circle around Clark and his wife.

The musicians are young and attractive, especially a girl named Christine who is wearing a yellow headband and playing a tambourine. We learn that the group, including the mandolin player but excluding the fiddler, is an out-of-work Toronto theatre company called the Ne'er-Do-Well-Thesps, and that there are more than thirty verses to the song they will be singing to the tune of 'Old Joe Clark' for the next four days:

Our Joe Clark he is a man,
Straight and tall and true,
He's the kind of man, you know,
Who'll do the best for you.

> Rally round our Joe Clark,
> Rally round I say,
> Rally round our Joe Clark,
> He will lead the way.

Clark, nervous and excited, is both smiling and perspiring. He is a tall, slim, well tailored, pressed and turned out man, and looks a bit silly in an open-necked shirt with a yellow scarf tied around his neck like a bib. The arrival of the musicians gives him something to do with his hands. He even attempts to dance a few turns, but it is an awkward, self-conscious effort.

Maureen McTeer is working the crowd.

"How's it going Mrs. Clark?" someone asks.

"Please call me Maureen."

"Well then, how's it going . . . Maureen?"

But she doesn't hear and has already moved on to shake the next outstretched hand.

One of us asks her whether she's having a good time. She says she is, it's been a little tiring for the past five months, but win or lose, an experience she wouldn't have missed. What about us? We tell her we are having a good time. Please call me Maureen, she says.

The crowd presses in every direction; they like the music and seem to like the company. There are, as they say, good vibes. But around Clark himself there seems to be an open space.

We find out why as we press to the centre of the room.

Spread-eagled flat in the middle of the floor is a television cameraman, and creeping along the fringes of the crowd like a Viet Cong guerrilla moving through a rice paddy, is a sound technician.

Clark is almost straddling the cameraman. He is shooting nervous glances at the floor, where the cameraman is constantly squirming for a different angle.

And Now a Word from John Bassett

The media were everywhere at this convention, and they missed nothing—or at least nothing trivial.

Television is, of course, the king of the media. And it was therefore the dominant element in the theatrical event that was the leadership convention. The influence of television on the convention was evident on several levels. One aspect was expressed by Toronto *Star* columnist Richard Gwyn:

Political conventions and television, it goes without saying, feed upon each other. "Camera angles" have dictated the layout inside Ottawa's Civic Centre. All the dramatic events, such as the tributes to former prime minister John Diefenbaker and to retiring leader Robert Stanfield, and the speeches by and the "spontaneous" demonstration for each candidate, as well as the final ballots, have been scheduled for prime time.

None of this is new. Even the New Democrats do their best to be dull, yet still make these bows to media necessity.

The difference is that for the first time in the history of the Conservative party, television has become not just the structure of the convention but its substance.

Perhaps an even more fundamental reflection of television's becoming the very substance of the convention was the choice of television commentators:

—David Crombie, who took a flyer at the leadership himself, but finally settled in as a key Flora MacDonald supporter.

—John Bassett, long one of the Tory heavy hitters, who donated $5,000 to the financially bankrupt Wagner campaign.

—Eddie Goodman, Tory bagman and a power in Flora MacDonald's campaign.

—John Robarts, who also took a fling at the race, and despite its failure is still a major factor within the Tory party.

—Dalton Camp, a man known also to have had some dealings with this convention.

All these people did much to write the scenario for the convention, then served as critics and presented the Canadian people with their ready-formed perceptions of what was happening.

This convention saw the complete merger of the dominant medium with the event.

This merger of observers and participants was also brutally one-sided. There is credence to the complaints of Jack Horner, Heward Grafftey and Patrick Nowlan that they were sandbagged by the media. All the television commentators represented one side of the party—the winners. Conservative journalists such as Peter Worthington and Lubor Zink of the Toronto *Sun* were literally frozen out. Yet the editorials and columns of the *Sun* were far more reflective of the gut feelings and mood of the Conservative party than the commentators on the networks. But the fix was on.

Another effect of the absolute dominance of television was the

virtual elimination of the middlemen—print journalists—who
were left with several options, none of them terribly satisfactory:
    (a) Sitting in the press room watching television.
    (b) Tracing all forms of trivia (for colour side-bars).
    (c) Interviewing each other and swapping rumours.
    (d) Trying to become pundits.
    Punditry is generally seen as the best of these options. The
treadmill to oblivion appears to move slower, and besides some
of the more fortunate of the pundits may make it onto the Teevee.

Jack Horner

Thursday

He's Looking Good — He's Looking Good

Thursday morning a Brian Mulroney press conference is the only show in town. The Candidate smoothes into the conference room. Suit by Brisson & Brisson; crisp shirt by changing it a lot; public relations by Beauregard, Landry, Nantel, Jasmin & Associés; baritone by birth; bilingualism by necessity; intimacy with press by design. He is on Christian-name terms with the vast majority of the reporters.

Just this very day, he announces, *Le Devoir* and *La Presse* have published editorials endorsing his candidacy.

Even we, suspicious as we are, find it hard to subscribe to the theory that these endorsements might have anything to do with the fact that as a member of the Cliche Royal Commission Mulroney provided *Le Devoir* with the most scoops it has had since the days of Henri Bourassa, or that *La Presse* is owned by Power Corporation, widely reported to be Mulroney's biggest corporate backer.

Geoff and Evelyn, Dick, Michel, Dave and Bob ask Brian a few questions.

"Well, Geoff, Evelyn, Dick, Michel, Dave and Bob, Canada is indivisible in two languages . . . We'll be spending about $175,000 raised in small contributions at fund-raising dinners . . . We didn't peak too soon—as John F. Kennedy put it, there's no such thing as peaking too soon . . . We won't disclose the money thing yet, because party rules say we don't have to, but as our financial chairman, David Angus, will be pleased to tell anyone, the biggest contribution was $10,000, from Paul Desmarais of Power Corporation, and we'll be giving details of all contributions over $1,000 within thirty days of the convention . . . No, I don't expect to be a kingmaker, I expect to be a king . . . I had no knowledge of any trust fund that might have been established for Mr. Wagner . . . And, yes, really, all candidates deserved two minutes for elbowing during the nominating meetings . . . Thank you, ladies and gentlemen."

Brian and his friends breast their way through the crowd, leading with the chin, and bump into Laurier Lapierre, the historian turned losing NDP candidate turned talk-show host.

"Brian, may I have ten minutes with you?"

"Of course, Laurier, just talk to my man here. You're the guy I wanted as a candidate in '72."

Laurier is granted ten precious minutes, and The Candidate and his entourage sweep off to the next spontaneously delirious reception.

It is not surprising that Mulroney should have been the only candidate to call a convention press conference. He has been assiduously courting the press for fifteen years, and has become a master of manipulating it.

Mulroney first gained widespread recognition in Quebec in 1974 and 1975 as a member of the three-man Cliche Commission into violence in the construction industry. The commission exposed a story of loan-sharking, unions dominated by criminals, and corruption at the highest levels of the Bourassa government. Much of the information saw the light of day because one member of the commission was a master of the judicious leak.

Mulroney's career as a top labour lawyer and activities as a Tory organizer had brought him many press contacts. He really flowered on the Cliche Commission, when he had the hottest information in the province to give out. And give he did, principally to *Le Devoir*, which beat out other papers day after day with hot front-page stories under the byline of Michel Roy. Other newsmen, perhaps with a greenish tinge, remarked that it's a good thing Roy is able to take dictation. Those others got their snippets too, and duly splashed them over their own front pages. A lot of journalists were heavily indebted to Brian Mulroney when he turned up as a candidate for the Tory leadership.

Paul Hellyer is scheduled to address an audience of Young Progressive Conservatives on the subject of macroeconomics. He arrives late and seems preoccupied throughout the lecture.

"How many of you think inflation is inevitable?" he asks.

The answer is unanimous—it isn't inevitable.

"What has been the rate of growth of the Gross National Product over the past few years?"

Nobody seems to know.

Hellyer gets his biggest applause when he notes that wage increases have depreciated investments.

Hellyer asks, "How many think the poor should have a better break?"

No hands go up.
"You're more conservative than I thought."
Everyone laughs.
But it is a listless meeting. Outside the room there is a gathering of Hellyer supporters and a group of country musicians. They prepare to move into the room as Hellyer finishes.
"All right boys," prompts an organizer, "let's hit 'em with a real zinger!" They move toward the open door, but they are stopped. Hellyer isn't finished yet.

In the corridor we briefly interview a young delegate from Ottawa. She is a Hellyer supporter, but her support of Hellyer is not as strong as her dislike of Mulroney. In this regard, her approach to the selection of a new leader is rather typical. Most delegates appear to start from the candidates they dislike and eliminate, in ascending order, until they are left with three or four candidates who are acceptable.
The interesting thing about this process of selection is that the delegates seem quite prepared to cross the ideological barrier that we have been told separates Hellyer, Stevens, Wagner and Horner from Mulroney, MacDonald, Clark and Fraser.
The young lady from Ottawa illustrates the eclectic reasoning to which the process is subject. She likes Hellyer, but can't understand his economic theories (fair enough). She will never vote for Mulroney because (a) he didn't find the time to speak to her club during the campaign, and (b) he made his pregnant wife stand for hours in a hospitality suite.
"That tells me an awful lot about his character."
She also thinks highly of Heward Grafftey and is considering voting for him on the second or third ballot.
We suggest that if she is considering a vote for Grafftey, she may be well advised to vote for him before the third ballot.

Split-second choreographed Mulroneymania is in full swing in the Château lobby as the Grafftey entourage arrives for the first stop of a triumphant tour of Heward's hospitality suites. Heward, three aides and one of us enter through the side door, and ride the elevator to Suite 481. There is nobody there but the bartender.
Phone calls are made, and we learn that there has been a change of plan, and the Grafftey partisans are gathering at the next stop, Suite 1919 at the Skyline. Riding over there, Grafftey explains how his campaign has been underestimated, and how he is certain of 225 Quebec votes on the first ballot.
Heward has a truly frightful case of thousand-yard-stare, and

his forehead is sweating profusely. It doesn't help when we arrive at 1919 to find the door locked.

"I'll go and get the key," says an aide, heading for the stairs.

"Why bother," says Heward, "Forget about the suites, nobody's coming. We'll just do the lobby of the Holiday Inn."

As we walk through the tunnel connecting the two hotels, a couple of people recognize the MP for Brome-Missisquoi. "Poor Heward," they say.

Heward stares straight ahead. His gears are obviously slipping fast. We take our leave.

"Thank you, Mr. Grafftey, I must run. I'd like to talk to you later, if possible. Could we have another appointment?"

"Yes, of course. Thank you for all I've done."

Heward Grafftey is the most successful Tory in Quebec, and the province's Torydom hates him for it. He says that he committed the ultimate Tory sin — getting elected. He has been in the House of Commons for fourteen of the past eighteen years, since he first made it, an Anglophone in a French riding, in the 1958 Diefenbaker Sweep. Heward works hard for his constituency. He's also the only person in this country with chronic Graffteymania.

He wants to get Trudeau out of office and keep blacks out of Canada. The free world is at stake. He explains his obsession with running for office by saying that "unlike the Asiatics we're competitive." A rumour in Tory circles explains it differently. We were told that he can only collect the income from his inheritance if he holds public office, or is running for it. It's one of the more gentle stories that Tories tell about Heward, and one of the few that aren't true.

Quebec's most successful Tory doesn't get any help from his supposed friends. In the 1972 election, when Claude Wagner got a $300,000 trust fund and plenty of campaign dough besides, the party contributed $1,200 to the Grafftey machine. He went through the entire campaign without mentioning Robert Stanfield or Claude Wagner. A grateful party cut back his allocation from the war chest.

When the dust had settled, Grafftey and Wagner were the only two Tories elected in the province. The Quebec caucus wasn't talking to each other. Grafftey and Wagner still don't talk to each other, except for public displays of party unity.

Heward was the first candidate to announce for the leadership, and ran hard from July, 1975, until the convention. It cost him more than $100,000. He says he hasn't spent any of his own money on the campaign.

In 1974, Grafftey declared his net worth as a quarter of a million dollars, most of it from holdings in the family's Consumers Glass Co. If it's true he didn't spend any of it on his leadership bid, he's obviously in a bit of a financial bind. Mulroney's men seemed to think so too.

One day, before the convention, Heward had a visit in his office from a Mulroney bagman. The bagman placed a cheque for $5,000 on the desk, a campaign contribution. Whom, he wondered, would Heward support when he was knocked out in the early balloting? A hypothetical question, said Heward, he was going to win, his poll proved it. Be realistic, where will your support go? More gesturing, glassy-eyed staring and desk-banging, and the same story. Heward was going to be the next leader of the Tory party. "Too bad," said the bagman, picked up the cheque, put it back in his pocket, and left.

Heward also confirms a story about a call he got on Sunday morning, before voting began. A man claiming to be David Angus, Mulroney's chief fund-raiser, called his room in the Château Laurier, and offered to pick up an estimated deficit of about $20,000 in Heward's campaign fund if Heward would throw the weight of his support behind Mulroney. That somebody called Grafftey is clear, but whether or not it was Angus isn't. Angus himself denies it. In the end it doesn't matter. The five delegates who came to Ottawa with Grafftey wearing his orange-and-blue badges voted for Mulroney anyway.

Other highlights of Grafftey's career include being a delegate to the United Nations Assembly in 1958 and 1966; putting his name to a book called *The Senseless Sacrifice: A Black Paper on Medicine*; and running around the country exposing defects in the automobile industry. He calls Ralph Nader the American Heward Grafftey.

He was the only person at the convention who thought he had a chance.

Later we witness the Apple Bust in Patrick Nowlan's suite in the Château Laurier. Nowlan is passing out apples, but this is, according to his brother, against the rules as all food must come from the hotel's kitchens. Some purposeful-looking hotel employees come to cart the illegal apples away. Apparently the Skyline Hotel isn't interpreting the rules as strictly because Annapolis Valley apples with a wrapper bearing a rather strange caricature of Patrick Nowlan are very much in evidence there.

We can't, however, find Patrick Nowlan. He is said to be off somewhere playing squash.

Meanwhile, the rumours build, multiply and divide.

If there is a lot of backroom dealing being done, as many of the rumours suggest, it seems at this stage a rather pointless exercise. All evidence suggests that the majority of delegates are either totally uncommitted or so "soft" in their commitment that the convention could go in almost any direction. No political trend has taken shape and no candidate has really emerged from the pack, with the possible exception of Mulroney, but even here the frenetic activity does not obscure a note of desperation.

If there is anything at this stage that is noteworthy in the mood of the delegates it is that the front runners — Hellyer, Wagner and Mulroney — also ring high on the unacceptability scale. That is, a typical response will be, "I can consider Clark and I can consider Sinc but I'll never vote for Wagner." Or "Hellyer is my first choice and I could vote for Clark or Flora but never Mulroney." At this point few delegates are ready to admit they will never vote for a woman, and those who will admit it generally are women themselves.

Nowlan, Fraser, Gillies and Grafftey are clearly going nowhere. Stevens, MacDonald, Horner and Clark are very much alive. Up front are Mulroney, Hellyer and Wagner.

If no bandwagon is developing for any candidate, there is a consensus shaping as to what the delegates want the party to represent and the image they want the new leader to convey. Personality is not the main issue and the convention is ready to consider almost any one of the candidates but only in the context of policy. Meanwhile, the more perceptive leadership hopefuls are trimming and altering their speeches and pitches to the delegates, and everybody wants to hear more.

Downstairs in the Bytown Lounge, Jack Horner has taken over and is working the floor. He is doing remarkably well considering the mean and abrasive style he adopted in the campaign. He is surrounded not only by a small band of true believers but by a group of attentive uncommitted delegates. An old couple from Alberta are naturally — if not quite logically — debating whether to vote for Clark or Horner on the first ballot. They are determined to see one or the other Albertan through to the end. Then they will reluctantly vote for either Wagner or Hellyer — anything to stop that Mulroney man who reminds them so much of the hated Trudeau. (On Sunday they would be sitting uneasily, with Clark buttons on their jackets, as John Diefenbaker made his last walk over to Claude Wagner.)

Some Hellyer supporters we met earlier now tell us that they are willing to "give Jack the first vote."

Much was made of Brian Mulroney's lack of parliamentary experience, and in an indirect way it may have cost him the leadership, but it didn't prevent him from being seriously considered by a large number of delegates. The rap against him would have had more force except that parliamentary experience was not exactly a strong suit of most of the other candidates either. Six of them — Joe Clark, Sinc Stevens, Claude Wagner, Jim Gillies, John Fraser and Flora MacDonald — had been in the House only since 1972, and of those only Wagner had previous provincial experience. The candidate who made the most of his parliamentary experience, Paul Hellyer, was hampered somewhat by the fact that almost all of it had been gained in the ranks of the Liberal party.

There was, however, one candidate who had had a long — eighteen years — and rather distinguished parliamentary career, all of it as a Conservative. He had been a prominent spokesman for his party since the mid-sixties. In the divided parliament that followed the 1972 election, he had been chairman of the Commons transport committee. Jack Horner looked at the other candidates and decided that he, more than any of them, *deserved* to be leader.

In his public appearances Horner is often seen to be angry, which is both part of his character and a useful device. During the leadership campaign most of his anger was directed at two targets. One was Joe Clark, the young upstart from the next riding, whose candidacy prevented Horner from going into the convention with a united bloc of western delegates behind him and having a good shot at the top prize — or at least so Horner and his supporters felt. There was more than the usual amount of wishful thinking in that proposition — even such a conservative Conservative as Sean O'Sullivan characterized Horner as the second most divisive possible leader the party could choose, after Flora MacDonald — but still it was widely believed. Only one member of the Alberta cabinet declared for Horner and that was his brother Hugh. The other ministers who declared all declared for Clark.

The other target of Horner's anger was the press, as the reporter to whom he tried to deliver a nationally-televised punch during the balloting found out. Horner feels that the press has been consistently unfair to him, a charge that is not without justice. Horner's demeanour, his Alberta ranch and his right-wing views lead to an easy caricature of him as a gun-toting, quick-shooting cowboy, riding off by himself into the sunset. But Horner showed a grasp of issues during the leadership campaign that was matched perhaps only by Clark, and his positions were generally less simplistic than those of most of the other candidates, 'right-wing' and 'moderate' alike.

Back in the mid-1960s Horner was a vigorous parliamentary critic of a scheme to set up a Bank of Western Canada, an enterprise that was headed by a Toronto financier named Sinclair Stevens. He expressed doubt about the financial soundness of Stevens' Bay Street empire, and demanded assurances from him that the bank would serve the west as a public utility. Both in the Commons Finance Committee and on the floor of the House he made strong speeches questioning whether Stevens' Westbank would be the genuine western Canadian bank westerners wanted. During the leadership campaign, at an all-candidates meeting in Toronto, Sinc Stevens fielded a question about the high profits of the chartered banks and cheerfully defended them, saying that high bank profits were good for the country. Jack Horner, sitting beside Stevens, took issue with him and said that the banks were an effective monopoly that didn't operate in the public interest.

Horner also has a well-developed talent for making enemies, and the campaign speech of his that got the most press was one in which he bad-mouthed all the other candidates except Dr. Richard Quittenton. Paul Hellyer "is hailed by some as a new messiah. But he is not new to the political scene and he is no Conservative messiah." Flora MacDonald "would like to be seen as the Canadian Margaret Thatcher. She is as much like Margaret Thatcher as Jack Horner is like David Lewis." Claude Wagner "entered the Conservative party, *and apparently was paid for* . . . ." Of Brian Mulroney he said that "the Power Corporation couldn't buy Argus and I promise that it can't buy Canada either," and of Sinc Stevens he asked, in reference to Westbank, "is our party so bankrupt in its ideology, talent and resources that it would entrust its leadership to a man who has already led so many Canadians down a ruinous road?" There was little to argue with in what Horner said (which perhaps blunted the reaction to the speech) but one could question the propriety of his having said it. Horner included the speech in his campaign brochure, just to make sure everybody knew he had meant what he said, along with newspaper attacks on his opponents as well as the usual puff-pieces on himself.

But if Horner has made enemies, he has made a large number of friends too, and his first-ballot total of 235 votes, which caught so many people by surprise, was a tribute to the extent to which he was able to cash in on those friendships. The Horner support was quiet, and included many people who simply felt that they owed one vote to good old Jack. One prominent Mulroney supporter, a former MP, said that he was still tempted to vote for Horner on the first ballot because he had had the next office to him in Ottawa and really liked the guy.

Meanwhile, the rumors build, multiply and divide.

At Sinclair Stevens' suite comfort is being taken in a remark by Brian Mulroney earlier in the day that his private poll had placed himself first (of course) and Stevens second.

Over cheese and a dreadful fruit punch, the host on our right keeps repeating: "He's looking good—he's looking good—he's looking good." On our left another Stevens operative is talking more to the point: "If it's true it is good news . . . but not surprising." "He's looking good—he's looking good," adds the other. "Yes," says the man on our left, "Sinc is doing quite well . . . God-dammit Reg, we're the only ones drinking this lousy punch."

Meanwhile the rumours build, multiply and divide.

There are endless permutations between Stevens, Wagner and Hellyer. We meet a friend who tells us that she has just had a drink with a woman whose husband had earlier been drinking with a friend who had a friend who had recently had supper with a friend of the John Turners—THE JOHN TURNERS— and the word is, Flora and Wagner have done a deal.

In the afternoon, Mulroney has what is billed as a meeting with Manitoba delegates. Premier Frank Moores of Newfoundland is picked out of the crowd and brought to the podium. Moores speaks about the need for new leadership and similar things, and then seems to grope for words for just a moment. "I wasn't supposed to say this until Saturday," he says, "but what the hell, I'll say it now—I'm supporting Brian Mulroney."

Mulroney has a button waiting for him and pins it to Moores' lapel. The cameras record the event and everybody applauds. Mulroney asks if there are any other provincial premiers in the room and everybody laughs.

As the meeting breaks up we look to see how many Manitoba delegates are present (we find three) and in the process we meet a couple from Quebec. The lady has atrocity stories of how Wagner has packed the Quebec delegation. "But that's finished," says the man. "Now we are meeting together for the first time and telling each other our experiences and I want to tell you, people are pretty fed up with what Wagner did. And I'm an old friend of his . . . In fact such an old friend they all thought for sure I

to be a party maverick. His record of support for social welfare measures is as consistent as that of any politician in the country. His reputation as a defender of civil liberties in general and the rights of ethnic minorities in particular developed over many years in the political wilderness of the prairies, and it was earned.

Nevertheless, when all is said and done, John Diefenbaker was never a radical and the opposition to him came from the "Ontario Establishment" of the party for the solid reason that they never thought he could win a general election. The successive leaders of the party—Dr. Manion with his tenuous tie to French Canada, Bracken with his image of Progressivism and George Drew with his glaze of sophistication—always seemed like possible winners.

But by 1956, there was nobody except Donald Fleming and Davie Fulton standing in Diefenbaker's way to the leadership, which is to say there was nobody at all. Who was to know that this was the season when, as George Grant wrote, Canadians were finally to protest "not against the principles but against the pin-pricks of the Howe regime?"

Dalton Camp claims he could sense the country was ready for George Drew. This is unlikely because while it is basically true that governments defeat themselves—our history is studded with the most unlikely premiers and mayors who happened to be in the right place at the right time—opposition parties that defeat governments generally at least project a fresh image. This was something George Drew couldn't and didn't do. John Diefenbaker did.

In the two-part general election that gave him first his minority and then his thumping majority, Diefenbaker proclaimed the possibility of a different Canada. A vision. A vision that made one think of the future in the romantic terms of a pioneering past. Ask someone today why he supported Diefenbaker and the first answer will be, "because he believed in the same kind of Canada as I did." Press on, and the answers will range from blank stares, through "he stood up for the country" to "he was the small guy taking on the big guy"—the ethic that unites the prairie homesteader of 1900 with the small-town dry cleaner of 1976. On one memorable occasion we were told that John Diefenbaker embodied the real conservative tradition that made Ontario what it is today—the nexus of the faithful worker and the paternalistic boss.

That John Diefenbaker could be, even for such a brief period of time, all things to all Canadians is a tribute to the imaginative

Heward Grafftey, Jim Gillies, Pat Nowlan and John Fraser

powers of the Canadian people as well as to the persuasive
powers of the Man Himself.

In office, the Diefenbaker government proved as conventional
as any of his predecessors, distinguished primarily by the colos-
sal incompetence of most of his ministers and by his own inabil-
ity to do anything but speak. Diefenbaker, according to his jaun-
diced critic Pickersgill, believed that when he said something he
did it. Thus during the Diefenbaker ministry Canadians saved
themselves by building fallout shelters, liberating the Ukraine
and "getting tough with the Yanks."

The Diefenbaker legend is the subject of numerous books,
and more are in the works. Individually they tend to be rather
trying, but as a genre they are absolutely fascinating. They
chronicle and interpret every major and minor thought and
action. There is no need to add further to the growing literature
on the Diefenbaker legend here. But because Diefenbaker never
fully accepted the leadership of Robert Stanfield, and because he
has politically survived his successor, there is one aspect of the
legend that is still germane. This is that Diefenbaker was
betrayed by his own party.

John Diefenbaker won the loyalty (to the extent that the term
has meaning in politics) of the Progressive Conservative party
when he won the 1957 and 1958 elections. He lost that support in
stages as he lost his ministry in stages. That Diefenbaker won
and lost support so fast lends credence to the notion that he fell
victim to a plot—a plot of the same monied interests that tried to
prevent him from reaching office in the first place. In fact, however, the loss of support was so hasty because the Diefenbaker
government fell apart almost as soon as it was strung together.

But because Diefenbaker did not go gently into that good
night as all losing politicians must, the process of getting him out
was both messy and protracted.

Diefenbaker was given repeated stays of execution because
the Liberals under Lester Pearson appeared to be as inept and
implausible as the Tories. Inconclusive election followed inconclusive election as two of last century's warriors clutched and
clawed their way to the last hurrah. But Pearson knew when to
leave. Diefenbaker, with his Messiah complex, didn't.

Finally the Conservative party took a decision to hold a leadership convention. At its 1966 annual meeting it resolved "that
this party expresses its support of the Right Hon. John G. Diefenbaker, its national leader, and acknowledges its wholehearted
appreciation of his universally recognized services to the party;
and in view of the current situation in the party directs the
national executive, after consultation with the national leader, to

call a leadership convention at a suitable time before January 1st, 1968."

The convention was held, not quite over Diefenbaker's dead body — he assured his supporters after the leadership resolution was carried that he was only going to lie down and bleed awhile — but over his scarred and wounded body at least.

And so the idea or rather myth that Conservatives have some kind of death wish and that it is only their own perfidy and duplicity, expressed in an unquenchable thirst for their own leaders' blood, that keeps them from office became firmly rooted in our folklore. Typical of this is the following from MP Robert Coates' book, *The Night of the Knives:* "The Conservative Party of Canada is infamous for the wanton destruction of its leaders in times of adversity. Bennett, Meighen, Manion, Bracken [he skipped Drew] and Diefenbaker were victims of this suicidal addiction in recent years."

But it's history now. And indeed it would have been buried if Stanfield hadn't blown his chance.

Diefenbaker is ready. It is as if he has been priming himself for this moment, shaping and mentally writing his speech, since 1967. Indeed he has, over the past few weeks, been testing the speech in out-of-town tryouts in the Maritimes. Now it is opening night, on the big stage, and the old man is up for it. The lines are excellent, the timing is superb. Even the shaking jowls add to his display of power and conviction.

The speech is vintage Diefenbaker, a sliding, rolling, careening series of non-sequiturs. He grants forgiveness to Paul Hellyer and gets off a backhanded swipe at Brian Mulroney by saying that the leader should have years of parliamentary experience behind him (someone comments later that he was thinking not of Mulroney but of the fact that Gladstone was still Prime Minister at eighty-five). He lashes out at Trudeau and he lashes out at Castro, and it isn't clear whether he is angrier at Trudeau for going to meet Castro or at Castro for meeting Trudeau.

The bitterness of Diefenbaker's attack on Trudeau places the Trudeauphobia of the Conservatives at the centre of the convention. The naked fear and hatred of the Prime Minister that informs the entire gathering is articulated and crystallized in Diefenbaker's speech.

The speech also plays on another theme, and crystallizes something else among the delegates — the feeling that not only must the Trudeau government be beaten for the sake of Western civilization but that it is also, if not quite on the verge of collapse, vulnerable.

(This had its dangers. The spark of confidence that they were choosing the next Prime Minister which Diefenbaker ignited among the delegates may have shifted their mood away from candidates such as Hellyer and Stevens who suited their ideological outlook to others whom it was easier to imagine beating Trudeau — an outcome the Chief and his cronies wanted not at all.)

Someone notices that the roof is leaking. Either that or the sky is falling.

Diefenbaker launches into the worst French he can muster. He talks about how proud he is of having introduced simultaneous translation into the House of Commons. Claude Wagner squirms a bit as if suddenly his shorts are too tight.

"Bilingual cheques are next," someone says.

"Et dj'ai auterisay," says Dief, "pour la premeer fois dans l'histoire canadiyenne, les tcheques bilingues pour la fonctione publique."

"What more do you bastards want?" murmurs a political columnist sitting behind us. The *Le Jour* correspondent, sitting beside him, doubles over with laughter.

In the late 1960s, an important aspect of the revitalization of the Progressive Conservative Party, at least in the minds of Dalton Camp and his associates, was the establishment of a viable political position in Quebec.

Toward this end, a "Tory thinkers conference" was held in Montmorency Falls, Quebec, in August 1967. Among its proposals was the following: " . . . that Canada is composed of the original inhabitants of this land and the two founding peoples (deux nations) with historic rights, who have been, and continue to be joined by people from many lands."

The beauty of this resolution was in the eye of the beholder. It said to French Canada that the Tories, with their new saviour Marcel Faribault, were a party to be taken seriously. To English Canada, where Quebec was a matter of some concern and considerable puzzlement (these were the days of the Royal Commission on Bilingualism and Biculturalism and the Confederation for Tomorrow Conference, Ontario Tory Premier John Robarts' fling at statesmanship), it said that it was all a semantic misunderstanding.

The whole affair puffed new life into John Diefenbaker. The resolution was to be brought before the convention the Tories had organized to dispatch him. Diefenbaker threatened to withdraw from the convention with his supporters and thus cause an open split in the party (such was his standing at that time that most of the Tory brass considered the threat relatively empty) and it was quickly negotiated that the propositions from the Montmorency Conference would be merely tabled instead of adopted. William Davis, who was assigned to push the resolution through, quickly changed his speech. And with only Charlotte Whitton from Ottawa screaming bloody murder from the floor, the deed was done.

Diefenbaker then announced he would run to retain his leadership in defence of his position. In a speech that drew catcalls from Quebec, cheers from Alberta and bewildered stares from almost everywhere else, the Chief played on everyone's paranoia, talking about Berlin Walls and Checkpoint Charlies — and went out on the third ballot.

Robert Stanfield, who eventually emerged as leader, was thus hobbled with a non-policy that became all the murkier as he tried to explain (a) what it meant (b) that it really didn't exist. This was the first indication of just how accident-prone Robert Stanfield was when it came to high politics. This was also the first indication of how sweet life was to become for John Diefenbaker as he danced in front of his new leader all the way from Toronto in 1967 to Ottawa in 1976, covering his path with banana peels instead of rose petals.

The Liberals had a better idea: they invented Pierre Elliott Trudeau.

During this campaign the Tories demonstrated that their heart was in the right place as far as Quebec was concerned by zapping the candidacy of Leonard Jones.

"Many of my friends are French-speaking," said Leonard Jones at a Montreal news conference a couple of weeks before the convention. "Allegations that I am a bigot are false and unsubstantiated."

Jones was still hoping that he might find his way onto the ballot, despite the party's rejection of his candidacy in January. He had made his name as Mayor of Moncton, N.B., by taking a courageous stand against the use of French by the city's French-speaking population. A measure of his conspicuous lack of bigotry is that during his tenure patients in old-age homes were forbidden to speak their mother tongue amongst themselves.

He was expelled from the Progressive Conservative Party by Stanfield during the 1974 campaign, when Jones was running for a seat in Parliament on his one issue — opposition to bilingualism. His slogan was "Jones is Right". He beat the approved PC candidate, and took his seat in Parliament as an independent.

His leadership bid began when a group of his supporters

voted him back into the party after a meeting of the Moncton
Conservative Association had been adjourned. Stanfield threatened to resign if Jones rejoined the Tory benchers, and an investigating committee decided that Jones was not a party member,
and therefore could hardly run for the leadership. Announcing
the decision, Michael Meighen said Jones was an "active non-
supporter" of the party.

The disqualification of Jones was another indication of the
Tories desperate desire to get back into Quebec.

At this convention the Tories are not uptight at all about
French Canada. Of course everybody out West hates Quebec but
that is Trudeau's fault (on Saturday Claude Wagner will say that
only a PC government could heal the legacy of hatred generated
by the Liberals' policy) and for tonight at least the whole
problem has been rendered absurd.

After Diefenbaker's speech, the bar opens and a band starts
playing on a small stage under the stands. They demonstrate a
political range that has not been evident elsewhere at the convention. They lead off with an IRA song, 'We're off to Dublin in
the Green', then introduce a tune that was written in Germany
in the 1930s, and follow it up with 'Poppa Piccolino' and an endless Italian joke that gets more obscene as it goes along.

The crowd loves it.

" . . . . And now, a song for the last of our ethnic minorities,
The French Canadians! Alouette!"

Et les cheques. Bilingues, that is.

We slip out in order to get downtown to meet some friends
where Ian Tyson and the Great Speckled Bird are giving their all
on behalf of some candidate or other. It is the wrong night, the
wrong hotel and probably the wrong band but it isn't all wasted,
because on the way out we are about the only people at the convention who catch Heward Grafftey's floor demonstration.

Heward and about ten supporters are making their way across
the floor when they notice all the people up ahead listening to
the gruesome band.

"Jesus," says one, "there's too many people in there for a
demonstration. Who needs the aggravation, let's go round the
back." They disappear into an empty corridor.

In the bar downtown, one of us cross-examines a young lady
dressed in Flora MacDonald terra cotta. It is getting late, the
bars are closing and all the hospitality suites have shut for the
night. But it is not too late for this one delegate to talk about
Flora, even though in five hours she has to be up to serve a Flora
MacDonald breakfast.

"If you believe in becoming politically involved," she is saying, "and if you think the only practical outlet is in one of the
two mainstream parties, then it's quite simple. Flora comes the
closest to expressing things that I feel."

"But why? How is Flora different from any of the others?"

"She's a woman . . . but that really isn't the reason."

"What is it?"

"She is the best of the bunch."

The discussion winds its circular way into a knot.

There is no shaking her from her conviction about Flora, nor
can she talk about that conviction in a way that really expresses
what she wants to say.

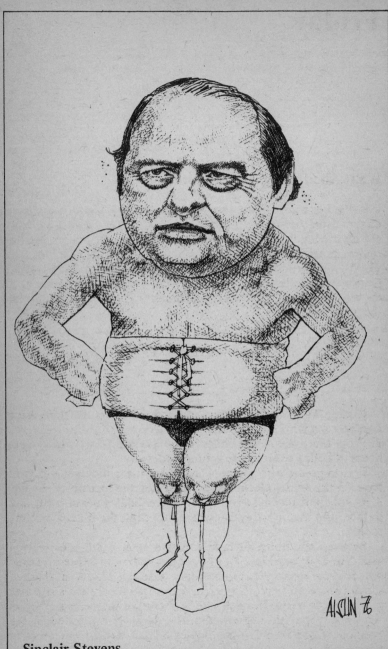

Sinclair Stevens

Friday

What About the Crow's Nest Pass?

For the diligent delegate the day begins early. There is a choice this morning between a campaign breakfast for Flora MacDonald and a breakfast hosted by the Conservative caucus. At the caucus breakfast a lucky Tory outbids the field to become, for $3,200, the proud owner of an autographed black-and-white photograph of Bob and Mary Stanfield. Another big moment is the rendition by Steve Paproski (Edmonton Centre) of a song for the outgoing leader:

> He's a gem, he's a smartie,
> And no matter, friend, what your party,
> He's your pal,
> He's your buddy,
> He's our Bob.

George Hees (Prince Edward-Hastings) pays $300 to have Paproski mow his lawn for half an hour.

From there the action shifts to the Skyline Hotel where eight hours of policy sessions are getting underway.

It is impossible to gauge what effect the policy sessions will have on the actual election. The most notable feature of the day is its apparent inconclusiveness. The candidates never meet face to face, and the crowd is fragmented through the hotel's meeting rooms.

Between the hours of nine and five each candidate is given four half-hour sessions. They speak according to a pre-arranged schedule on economics in one room, external affairs in another, social justice and social order in a third and political structures in the fourth room. If a delegate is interested in one topic he can simply stay put throughout the day. If he is interested in the position of one or a few candidates he can move from room to room.

There are few surprises in any of the speeches or answers.

Brian Mulroney causes a bit of a commotion when he speaks against the established caucus policy on nuclear reactor sales, and Joe Clark is reassuringly hawkish on foreign affairs. But for the most part, any reasonably conscientious delegate had plenty of opportunity during the campaign to hear from all the candidates — and these delegates were nothing if they weren't conscientious.

And most of the candidates come off well. (The press will report later than Clark forged ahead Friday because he wowed the delegates during the policy sessions, but his performance would have come as a surprise only to someone who hadn't seen him during the campaign.)

Moving from one session to another, we run into the Sinclair Stevens band, mostly high-school students from Southern Ontario. They're playing O-Bla-Di O-Bla-Da, and the boosters are having a hard time trying to fit the words to the music:

Who can do the job in the election race?
A man with en-er-gy to set the pace,
A man with great ideas and an honest face,
Put Sinclair Stevens in to do the job for you.
Put him in,
Put him in,
Put him in-n
Yes! He can do the job for you!
He can win,
He can win,
He can win-n,
Yes Sinclair Stevens is for you!

The tune has a tricky rhythm, and it's hard enough fitting the English words to it. The French version falls apart totally somewhere around the third line:

Choisissons un leader, choisissons Sinclair,
Un homme qui a du cran, un vrai meneur,
Un homme qui a du coeur, un homme de bon sens,
Car Sinclair Stevens est le champion du bon sens.
La victoire,
La victoire,
La victoi-re
Oui, Sinclair peut la décrocher.
La victoire,
La victoire,
La victoi-re
Pour l'avoir, il nous faut Sinclair.

In the middle of it all, surrounded by pimply trombonists and drummers, is the champion of good sense himself, Sinclair Stevens, doing a strange and spastic little victory dance with his wife, Noreen. According to rumours he has already made deals with all of the other eleven candidates, and he knows he is going to have to break ten of them.

Had we talked to Sinc Stevens when we went to his office in November and not to Don Blenkarn, we might not have received the same impression of the Stevens campaign as an uncompromising crusade for True Conservatism. Not that Sinc wouldn't have said the same things — he said them many times in the course of the campaign — but the tone in which he said them would have been different. Before entering politics he had built a multimillion-dollar empire on Bay Street, a place where one does not succeed by sticking to principles.

The high point of Stevens' financial career came on July 4, 1966, when the government granted a group headed by him a charter to start the Bank of Western Canada, which was to be the first new chartered bank in Canada since the 1920s. Westbank was the fulfilment not only of Stevens' personal dream, but also of a long-cherished hope of western Canada, which believed that a western-based bank, using western savings to build up western enterprises, could help build the west into an industrial region instead of a resource base for eastern and foreign interests. The presence of a Toronto financier, Stevens, at the head of such an undertaking could only lead to trouble.

As president of his bank Stevens had recruited the former governor of the Bank of Canada, James Coyne of Winnipeg, who after the row with Prime Minister John Diefenbaker that had driven him out of office had gone to work for Stevens' British Industrial Finance complex. Coyne was a westerner with strong opinions and a streak of unpredictable behaviour. He began to have misgivings about the Westbank scheme, and in February 1967 he went public with them. He said the bank was turning out not to be a truly western institution, and accused Stevens of siphoning money from Westbank to his other enterprises, which had encountered rough seas.

The dispute reached the Commons Finance Committee and the floor of the House. Opposition Leader Diefenbaker sided with his old enemy, Coyne, and accused Stevens of being in cahoots with his new enemy, Dalton Camp, who had recently succeeded in getting the party to call a leadership convention to replace him. Stevens denied Coyne's charges, and Camp denied

Diefenbaker's. The immediate crisis passed, but clearly Westbank wasn't big enough for both Coyne and Stevens. As it
turned out, it wasn't big enough for either of them.

In March Stevens lost control not only of Westbank but of the
whole BIF empire to one Marc Bienvenu, whose father had been
the first commissioner-general of Expo 67 and whose rapid rise
in Montreal financial circles paralleled Stevens' ascendancy in
Toronto. But it was beyond Bienvenu's power to rescue Westbank from the financial morass into which it had sunk, and a
few months later winding-up proceedings were begun.

For Stevens, the Westbank episode was only a temporary set-
back. Ambitious, irrepressible and still only forty, he had been a
journalist, a lawyer and the Boy Wonder of Bay Street. His
career was not over. In 1972 he contested York-Simcoe riding on
the fringes of Toronto and in the Tory surge in southern Ontario
defeated the incumbent Liberal, John Roberts. In 1974, as the
Liberals swept back all around him, he was re-elected with an
increased majority, and was named Tory finance critic.

It was from this position that he launched his campaign to
move the party to the right, attacking government spending and
"left-inspired welfarism." He saw the country moving with him,
and believed he was in possession of an idea whose time had
come. "And when it comes to the right to strike," he said in
December, "Oh boy! Last night I suggested to a student gathering that the next Conservative government should take a hard
look at the law which permits strikes in essential services — such
as the Post Office, nurses and the like. They said that was too
soft an approach. They wanted an end to this sort of thing by
overnight edict. To hell with reviews!"

But he too finally joined the rush toward the centre, and by
early February he was telling a Kitchener audience that he
wouldn't dismantle any existing government programs. Until the
convention opened he seemed like one of the candidates who
could come out of the pack and take it all, but in the early part
of the convention his hopes seemed to fade a little. Sinc Stevens
wasn't going to be Prime Minister, but he figured he could still
be Minister of Finance. And he was going to make sure of it.

A delegate is going about his business when he is pounced
upon by Heward Grafftey. Grafftey, who is being filmed, seizes
him by the Mulroney scarf, and, eyes goggling, forehead sweating, shouts:

"How can you do this to me . . . after all I've done for you?"

(David Ouellet had quit his $7,000 a year job as Grafftey's
special assistant a couple of weeks before the convention, to join

his brother Gary on the Mulroney campaign. Gary, a Quebec City lawyer, ended up in a bit of a hole after the convention was over, having spent tens of thousands of dollars of his own money renting office space for the Mulroney forces. It is going to be quite a long time before that favour is returned.)

There is a break for lunch. While Hellyer supporters are tucking into their Quebec ham and Manitoba coleslaw, Mulroneyites are gathering outside a Down East Luncheon in the Victoria Room of the Skyline. Here one of the key questions of the convention is answered. The no-free-booze rule is cracking. The Maritimers for Mulroney have flown in 24 cases of Newfoundland screech, and are giving it away to anyone wearing a Mulroney button. Fortunately Mulroney buttons are easy to rustle up.

All Mulroney suites are equipped with massive four-foot-square television screens the kind they have in superior taverns, so that Mulroneyites and curious passersby can catch great moments in The Candidacy. Slipping out to check on a few other lunches, we notice a sign by the TV, publicity for the firm that supplied the system:

> You Pay a Pretty Small Price for a Lot of Attention.

At the Wagner suite, there are a few sandwiches and no booze at all, let alone free stuff. The people, too, are a startling contrast. Male Mulroneyites all seem to be bronzed giants over six feet tall, while female ones are slender and elegant. Wagnerians of both sexes, on the other hand, all seem to be short and fat.

Heward Grafftey is ranting to a small crowd in Le Grand Salon, coping with 'The Economy — Priorities in Transition'. About half the crowd is wearing Mulroney scarves. As Horner supporters gather outside, Heward ends his question period on an up beat — the next Prime Minister of Canada must bring government back to the people, and that's just what he intends to do.

The room fills up for Horner, who gives a rousing speech with all the required ingredients — Sir John A., John George Diefenbaker, Robert Stanfield, Trudeau in Cuba, high government spending. Jack Horner has an interesting speech defect, the same one as Joe Clark — Diefshpeak. There must be a very wealthy speech therapist somewhere in Alberta teaching all the province's politicians to sound like the old man.

He doesn't think workers in the public sector should have the right to strike. In addition. . .

"I propose a law that will give innocent third parties the right to strike ... er ... I mean the right to compensation."

He gives as an example an apple grower whose produce rots because of a rail strike. He should have the right to sue the strikers for compensation. The example is clearly aimed at the maritime delegates, some of whom are still munching Nowlan apples, despite the Great Apple Bust. Horner answers a couple of questions about Maritime freight rates, the Come-by-Chance refinery and the Bricklin episode.

It seems that transport is the only issue that generates any serious questions. At every policy session, the candidates are asked lengthy technical questions about the Crow's Nest Pass agreement, or the difficulty of getting from St. John's to Charlottetown. Compromise stands on all other issues have been thrashed out and endorsed by all candidates a long time ago, but the delegates do want to know how much the guy on the stage knows about the iniquity of the freight rates he's paying under Trudeau Socialism.

Toward the end of the afternoon, by pure coincidence, all three members of the Last Post Outasight Team independently decide to hear what Doctor Q has to say about External Affairs.

Dr. Richard Charles Quittenton, candidate for the leadership of the Progressive Conservative party, is using the policy session to explain a scheme he has for turning trees into wood alcohol to use as fuel for automobiles. Curiously, Thursday's New York *Times* carried a story announcing that Mobil Oil Corporation has found a simple one-step process for converting wood alcohol into high-grade gasoline. About ten people are in the room, resting their feet, but there is one questioner.

"Doctor Quittenton, you've told us about the wood alcohol route, what about the sun and wind route?"

Covering this vital discussion of policy, besides the Last Post, is the correspondent for Hsinhua, the New China News Agency.

We ask him what he hears, and how he's enjoying the convention. He says it's pretty confusing, and he only just got in. He tells us that Hsinhua has a team of two reporters working the convention, and we wonder where the other one is.

He's covering Heward Grafftey.

The Man Who Never Was

When the policy sessions are over, all the candidates have said more or less the same things. They have all told the delegates, who like their conservatism straight and pure, what they wanted to hear. It is still an open question, however, whether what they want to hear is what they want to vote for. One candidate's poll of delegates reportedly said that while 80 per cent really wanted a leader clearly identified with the political right, only 20 per cent were prepared to vote for such a leader.

And despite the final convergence of all the candidates on policy, important differences remain. They are generally expressed in symbols, such as attacks on Dalton Camp. But what they amount to is nothing less than endorsement or repudiation of the leadership of Robert Stanfield.

In the wake of three successive defeats, it would have been naive to think that Stanfield would have the stomach or, indeed, be allowed to lead the party into a fourth general election. Under normal conditions, however, given the demoralized state of the party after losing an election it thought it was going to win, it would have been quite natural for Stanfield to continue to lead the party for a time in opposition, allowing time for the election dust to settle, for the aura of victory to wear from the Liberals and, above all, for some logical successors to emerge either within the caucus or from outside.

This was what Stanfield wanted. At the first meeting of caucus, attended also by the MPs who had been defeated in the election, he offered his resignation, expecting that he would be given a vote of confidence in return for an understanding that he would leave well before 1978. Peter Reilly, who had lost his seat in Ottawa West and was about as representative of the mainstream of the Conservative party as Fidel Castro, delivered an impassioned appeal to him to stay. But most of the people who might have been expected to support him were silent, perhaps because of their own ambitions.

The race for the leadership was on. The fact that the Tories went immediately from an election defeat into an open leadership struggle weakened their credibility as an opposition considerably, especially since, unlike the Liberal situation in 1956-57 after Louis St-Laurent resigned, there was no clear front runner. The Conservatives in Parliament created their own void. And they compounded their problems by appearing to thrash about in all directions for a saviour: to Alberta and, of all places, the Liberal cabinet.

But the major question was never which individual would eventually emerge as leader, but what political stance the party would take and what faction would gain control. All the candidates, willy-nilly, became identified on one or the other side of this question.

In the desperation that followed the 1974 defeat, compounded by the subsequent near-destruction of the Tory government of Ontario (a government which was seen by many Tories as the embodiment of Stanfield's policy — or rather Stanfield was seen as a creature of the quasi-Liberal government in Queen's Park), the mood was blue murder. The party had blurred its aims and principles, ran the arguments; it had drifted to the political left until it was no longer distinguishable from the Liberals. Now was the time to repudiate the Dalton Camps who had wrenched control of the party from the hands of John Diefenbaker and pushed it down the slippery slope.

The arguments at this stage were conducted through Camp on the one side and the Château Cabinet on the other. The Château Cabinet was a group within the caucus whose purpose, according to one of its members, Sean O'Sullivan, was to "reawaken interest in the philosophy and principles of conservatism." He saw it as being part of a process "something like Holy Year — Renewal and Reconciliation. We wanted people to stop and ask themselves, 'what am I doing in the Conservative party?' "

It also had a more practical goal, which was to influence, if not determine, the outcome of the leadership race. This was to be done not necessarily by openly supporting any one leadership candidate but by issuing a manifesto on which the candidates would be asked to state their position. However, it never got beyond a working document, which was written by Kim Abbott, a career civil servant sympathetic to the group, and which soon got leaked to the press.

"Our cultural objective," said the document, "will be a united and strong country created by the assimilation of all newcomers, and unassimilated pockets of long-time residents." This had several implications, one of which was that "the flow of immigrants to Canada must be geared to Canada's economic and cultural interests." In addition, "the future of Canada as a nation depends upon the settlement of regional differences and an end to the excessive demands of Quebec. As it may no longer be possible to negotiate a lasting settlement with Quebec under the British North America Act we must consider a New Federalism."

It was, as O'Sullivan is not slow to emphasize, a working document, and many amendments and additions were made to it before it finally disappeared into oblivion. To the extent that it represented the kinds of things that were being discussed within the right wing of the Conservative party, however, it startled many people, most of them Conservatives themselves. Dalton Camp, in his Toronto *Star* column, issued a strongly worded reply:

> Throughout the eight years of Stanfield's leadership, power in the party has been transferred from the party rank and file, from the national association and the constituencies, to the caucus — and thence from the caucus to a group within it. Stanfield and the moderates have exhausted themselves in efforts to reconcile the irreconcilable, to placate the implacable.
>
> Along the way, the party has lost its commitment and wavered in its purpose. Everything was done for compromise and conciliation, to keep the peace in the midst of a war of recrimination.
>
> But now that the party knows — unmistakably — what Sean O'Sullivan and the rest of the Château Cabinet stand for, how is reconciliation possible? Somewhere along the road to the convention, while the search is on for a leader, perhaps the party will find its courage. Failing that, who cares who leads it into oblivion?

Meanwhile, Camp himself became a thoroughly discredited figure within the party. The heat on him became so hot that even Peter Worthington, no Camp lover, felt obliged in the name of sanity if not fairness to defend him:

> If I were a Tory delegate, the candidate I'd be most impressed with would be the one who didn't disown, or treat Dalton Camp as a leper. It would be refreshing to hear, someday, a candidate admit to knowing or even having seen and chatted with Dalton Camp sometime within the past three to 10 years. Here's a guy, former president of the party, who has given years of service to what he believes in, and has helped and been associated with a number of the leadership candidates, yet who is considered to be political pariah by them all.

Of course, there are other interpretations one can put on Worthington's column — perhaps he was trying to smoke out the so-called Camp candidates. And this raises the question of Dalton Camp's influence on the party and the leadership campaign in particular.

Camp should be believed that he himself has very little influence on the Conservative party (perhaps with a few allowances made for the self-serving nature of his protestations of innocence). But since Camp has now become a generic term, his

influence survives in the form of the moderate political positions
he has advocated. Dalton Camp as an issue would not go away.
And this posed a serious problem for all the candidates who
were originally linked with Camp, one which they handled, with
one exception, not well at all.

At one time or another, Flora MacDonald, Brian Mulroney,
Joe Clark and John Fraser were all identified as Campites. One
of the scenarios most often heard in the early stages of the campaign was that Camp had money on all four which would be
parlayed onto one winner as the others gave way. It was said that
Camp had a hundred and fifty delegates who would abstain on
the first ballot and then go with whichever of the four looked
good. The response of the candidates was near-panic. Mulroney
claimed he hadn't seen or talked to Camp for years, Fraser took
refuge in a new ultraconservative image and was quoted as wish-
ing Camp would shut up, and MacDonald hemmed and hawed
and did a lot of sputtering. Joe Clark merely insisted that he was
his own man and that when the crunch came he would be more
acceptable to the other side than Flora or Brian. But nobody was
listening to Clark.

On actual policy matters, the issues within the party revolved
first around Quebec — both in terms of the implementation of
what under Stanfield had become a bipartisan policy on bilingualism and in the narrower terms of an approach to winning
support among voters in French Canada.

Jim Gillies threw the first grenade with a speech and subsequent article which explicitly rejected the Stanfield openings to
Quebec. Other candidates followed suit, notably Sinclair
Stevens, while Jack Horner was thundering in Parliament over
bilingualism. It was in essence a direct appeal to the anti-French
backlash in English Canada.

Other issues also arose — "law 'n' order," "abortion on
demand" — and everybody was against "big government."

Every candidate tried to stake out some turf on these issues —
except Brian Mulroney who, rather quixotically, attacked policy,
any policy, as the bane of the Tory party. He fooled nobody.

Interestingly, Joe Clark quietly identified himself with Robert
Stanfield throughout and chose the convention program, printed
as a tribute to Stanfield, to express his support again:

> Two weeks after the 1974 election I met a young French
> Canadian, who was still flirting with separatism, but had
> voted, in Quebec, on July 8, "for Robert Stanfield". He
> told me "your party started with two problems in my pro-
> vince. The first was respect — we didn't trust you. The

second was charisma. Mr. Stanfield made the Conservatives respectable in Quebec — and if I were a political party I would rather have a problem of charisma than a problem of respect."

Robert Stanfield took our leadership when we were divided internally and confined electorally to rural English Canada. People spoke of our past, not our future. He changed that, through policy development, candidate recruitment, and the steady construction of a reputation for responsibility. He made us a competitive, modern, national party.

For Stanfield, it was no doubt a welcome note, but it was also, as he was all too aware, a rare one.

Friday night is Stanfield Night. In the taxi taking us to the Civic Centre, we hear reports of a power blackout in the area of the city that includes the Centre, and pass street after street of darkened houses. The ultimate sandbag, we figure. But at the Centre itself all the lights are on.

As the arena fills, Stanfield Night begins with trivia. The candidates organize cheers of themselves as they make their entrances, and the half-attentive crowd gets to applaud as various leading lights of the party are introduced. The Wagner group is not yet up to full strength but it still gets off a lusty boo when Claude Dupras, president of the Quebec PCs is introduced. Dupras is supporting Mulroney. There is a film tribute to Robert Stanfield, the parts of which we catch cannot even rise to the level of being maudlin. But it is finally over and Peter Lougheed, Premier of Alberta, is called upon to introduce Stanfield. Lougheed doesn't even make the gesture of getting off at least one phrase in French, but his speech is generally well received by those who are listening.

It is Lougheed's only platform appearance of the convention, and it is noteworthy only for being so low-key. For this is the man who could, and in the minds of many Tories should have been the star of this convention.

Throughout the campaign, while the declared candidates were trudging around the country unsuccessfully trying to generate some excitement, there was a parallel search for a saviour who would put them all out of their misery. The search focussed on John Turner after his resignation from the cabinet (the highlight of the Turner-for-leader movement was a suggestion by Sinc

Stevens — always the realist — that Turner should cross the floor bringing twenty to twenty-five like-minded Liberals with him, thus causing the government to resign) but the Tory leadership couldn't match the attraction of a highly-paid Toronto law practice for the former finance minister. There was a brief flurry of interest in John Robarts. One Edmonton man had yet another idea:

"Maybe, just maybe, Ernest Manning could be persuaded to come out of retirement to serve this country as its leader. His experience, past record, the current esteem in which he is held by all who know him go far to quieten any apprehension I might have about his chances of winning the leadership and ultimately forming the next government of Canada."

But for the most part, Tories looking for a saviour looked toward the present and not the past occupant of the Alberta premier's office. As one Quebec Conservative organizer put it, "I'm taking the Buddhist position and praying for Peter Lougheed." That the man responsible for seventy-five-cents-a-gallon gasoline in Ontario, the blue-eyed Arab of Edmonton, was the answer to all of the party's electoral problems was a proposition whose truth was more obvious to committed Tories than to others. No less than the Turner, Robarts and Manning campaigns, the Lougheed campaign was a mark of desperation.

Nevertheless, the proposition was widely believed. No matter how many times Lougheed said he wasn't running, there were people who took each successive "no" to mean "maybe". Lougheed himself did not perhaps discourage such interpretations, but there is nothing he could have said that would have cooled his more zealous supporters. For the Lougheed campaign had its uses, even for those who were not themselves convinced that the premier would run. It gave people, as Joe Clark said, a fence to sit on. "I'm for Lougheed," was a typical answer to the question "who are you for?" in the months before the convention. If you persisted and asked, "and if Lougheed doesn't run?" you often got, "well, then I'm waiting to hear the speeches."

Sean O'Sullivan said that the Lougheed campaign was being manipulated by (who else?) Dalton Camp and his forces, who figured that as long as the prospect of a Lougheed candidacy could be kept alive, the other side wouldn't organize and potential candidates would be kept out of the race. It wasn't Lougheed's fault, O'Sullivan added; he was being used. In any case, in the end the man from Alberta meant exactly what he said.

Allan Fotheringham explained Lougheed's decision not to seek a position that was his for the asking by saying that he lacked the energy for it, that his recent election campaign had simply taken too much out of him. But that is rarely a determining factor for politicians — Ross Thatcher went into the 1971 campaign in Saskatchewan knowing that his heart could not take the strain, lost the election, and died a month later. A more convincing rationale was advanced by Clark, a political colleague of Lougheed's of many years' standing, who said that the premier lacked not the energy but the interest. Why give up almost unchallenged authority in Alberta to lead a party whose electoral prospects are, at best, questionable?

"He's got a lot of things started in Alberta that he wants to finish," said Clark. "The changes in Alberta are being called the Lougheed Revolution; if he leaves now it will be the Hugh Horner Revolution. When I travelled with him in the 1971 campaign, late at night on the road, he almost never talked about federal matters. Provincial matters are what interest him. He knows Alberta very well but he doesn't know the rest of the country in the same way. He would have to go through the same learning process nationally as he has provincially."

There were other people who could do the job in Ottawa. So Peter Lougheed was not going to discourage his good friend Joe Clark from seeking the leadership.

On the convention floor at the north end of the arena we are in a good position to see the Stanfield entourage enter. The demands of television are such that an entrance of this sort gives the appearance of being a Papal procession. With boom microphones arranged along the side like a lancers' honour guard and with the bright lights trained on the centre of attraction an aura, if not of saintliness, then at least of other-worldliness is created. The procession must move at a slow and stately pace, no faster than the cameramen can pace backward. On the fringe of the procession, there is turmoil as everyone with a portable tape recorder tries to joust with the pushers and shovers trying to clear a path for the stage party. Then come the cable bearers, gathering, moving and straightening the camera cables. Then the cameramen moving backward constantly trying to keep the man in focus. While everyone is shoving and tripping along the periphery of the procession, in the centre all is orderly. Stanfield, accompanied by his wife and daughter, moves straight ahead, pretending the cameras do not exist, and smiles and waves to the crowd, but only the cameras can see him and he can see nothing except the cameras.

Finally introduced and ready to go, Stanfield gets off a few jokes and then launches into his prepared speech.

It is a bittersweet occasion for Robert Stanfield. During the afternoon in the House there were kind, gentle and sometimes witty tributes paid to him on his last day as opposition leader. He answered them all with the self-deprecating grace of which he has always been capable and for which he has lately become known. And tonight in the crowded arena, in spite of the acrimony that has swirled around his leadership — even today the corridor gossip continues as if this convention was merely a reconvening of the 1967 struggle in which he defeated Diefenbaker — everyone is here to listen to him and to pay him his tribute.

But the simple fact is that Stanfield is leaving because he was defeated. No matter what the extenuating circumstances, Robert Stanfield blew it three times in a row, and he blew it because he did a lot of dumb things.

In any case, tonight, Stanfield is to speak for himself. He has to do more than give a graceful farewell: he has to defend himself and what he considers to be the best interests of the Progressive Conservative party.

While getting a few shots off at Diefenbaker, the main burden of Stanfield's speech is a defence of the two-party system and an appeal for moderation within the Conservative party.

"Some wish," he says, "to pile ideological confrontation and polarization on top of the tensions inherent in our country. I understand the attitude of a socialist who is committed to sweeping changes in our basic institutions, and who does differ ideologically from liberals and progressive conservatives. I understand the efforts of a socialist to ridicule liberals and progressive conservatives because we do not differ ideologically. But for a Conservative to take such bait and set out to establish ideological differences where none exist or ought to exist, to polarize this country and add to its inevitable tensions, let me say simply and without personal offence, that such a Conservative is misguided."

It is a new tone for this convention and, no doubt, a deliberate attempt to introduce some reason into the constant scathing attacks on what John Diefenbaker called "the Trudeau party." Up until now the impression has been created that as far as the system is concerned the Conservative party is the only legitimate one left. It is not enough merely to exchange seats in the House: the Liberals must be destroyed, root and branch. Not an alternative government but an ideological crusade has been demanded — and on prime television time. Stanfield's message is to cool it. He also suggests that they cool the right-wing rhetoric that seems to be an unavoidable feature of Conservative leadership campaigns and has pervaded this campaign even more than previous ones:

"Again, some of us wish to elevate a legitimate concern for individual self-reliance and individual enterprise into the central and dominating dogma and theme of our party. Why do we spoil a good case by exaggeration? Why do we try to polarize a society that is already taut with tension and confrontation? We are right to be concerned about the growth of government expenditures and about the dead weight of government on the active and the enterprising, but do we have to seem to be wearing blinkers so that we seem to neither see, understand, nor care about the problems of many Canadians? Surely our aim is a compassionate society as well as a prosperous economy."

It is an understated yet forceful speech, carefully reasoned and skilfully delivered, an expression of the graceful, moderately progressive Robert Stanfield who seems to have blossomed only since his last election defeat.

The new image that is being created around Stanfield must in part represent a certain desperation of his admirers. If he has no other saving grace as a politician or public figure, they seem to be saying, let's at least pass the word that he is a decent bloke. During the leadership campaign absolutely nobody who has had any dealings with the man would really get down on him, although in some cases there are grounds for suspicion that people were holding back. The worst even his political enemies within the party will say is that he is stubborn and unbending. For example, to some, Stanfield's decision to stick to his ill-conceived wage and price freeze reflected his stupid stubbornness (others ascribe it to lofty principle). He was also, we were told, rude to The Chief during his first months in office.

In any case there is no point talking about the "real" Stanfield, because as with every major politician there probably isn't one. We perceive the man only in images — and Stanfield has had several. First he was the rather right-wing banana-eating puppet of Dalton Camp. Then he was the incompetent boob who let the Grits hornswoggle him. Now he is the modest, decent man of principle with the priceless gift of a wit that whether turned toward himself or upon others does not cut or hurt. But the trouble with images, even when they are not artificially created, is that they tend to freeze and allow no room for change or growth.

And Stanfield has changed, and, indeed, grown. While he is

no doubt a beneficiary of the tendency of the media to make heroes of politicians after they are no longer in a position to do any harm, his recent transformation cannot be ascribed to that alone. Perhaps because of the struggles that have gone on constantly in the party under his leadership, sometimes openly and more often just below the surface, Stanfield has learned a few things since 1967. In his rejection of the idea that there had to or even should be a real difference between the Liberal and Conservative parties, he showed an appreciation of the purposes and methods of the two-party system that is rare among Canadian politicians.

When you ask them what the difference is between their party and the Liberals, Progressive Conservatives tend to talk about matters of style and circumstance rather than substance. "You can't tell an individual Tory from an individual Liberal," says Dr. Jimmy Johnston, "but you can tell a roomful of Tories from a roomful of Liberals. The Tories are all fighting with each other." Brian Mulroney says that "you don't get involved in a political party because of its ideology, but because there is a group of like-minded people in the party you feel you can work with."

In fact, there has been no clear political difference between the Liberal and Conservative parties since free-trade-versus-the-tariff stopped being the crucial issue in Canadian politics. It is questionable whether such a difference is even possible. The tendency for all parties to seek the Great Canadian Middle seems to be irresistible, and for that matter in almost all countries that practise some form or other of parliamentary democracy the lines between the competing parties become seriously fudged. Pierre Elliott Trudeau's election victory of 1974 was, after all, based on the electorate's rejection of wage and price controls, and Lyndon Johnson fashioned his 1964 landslide in the United States by promising peace in Vietnam.

There is a widespread feeling that there is something not quite kosher about this, that it is not strictly speaking the way the system is supposed to work. But it is arguable that not only can the parliamentary system work without there being any real political difference between the two major parties, but it is absolutely essential to the smooth functioning of the system that there be no such difference. A polite form of government in which everybody respects the wishes of the majority can work so long as political differences don't really matter. When they do begin to matter they are generally settled by other than electoral means, as the people of Chile found out to their chagrin not long ago. It

was a lesson that Salvador Allende, as dedicated a constitutional-
ist as he was a socialist, never had a chance to learn.

This is not to say that there are no distinctions to be made
between different parties or factions within parties, but only that
these distinctions must always be kept within bounds. In Canada
these bounds are represented by Social Credit on one side and
the NDP on the other. The relative tameness of the NDP when it
is in or near power is perhaps the best evidence for the existence
of these limitations. (None of this prevents the NDP from continuing to profess an Allende-like faith in the capacity of the system to accomplish change, a faith that puts their commitment to
the system on a completely different level from that of the Liberals and Conservatives, who only believe quite rightly in the
capacity of the system to preserve the status quo.)

While there is a certain purgative satisfaction in occasionally
throwing one crowd out of the East Block and putting in
another, there is little evidence that Canadians are crying out for
a 'real choice'. The reason Conservatives, this convention aside,
often play down differences of politics between themselves and
the Liberals is that there aren't any. In recent years the differences have been regional (an Alberta Liberal is about as common as a Montreal Tory), religious (the Liberals were Catholic
and the Tories Protestant at least as far back as when Sir John A.
Macdonald hanged Louis Riel), and to an extent social, but now
even those distinctions are breaking down: the three Tories who
turned out to be the leading candidates for the party leadership,
Claude Wagner, Brian Mulroney and Joe Clark, are all Cathol-
ics. The most important difference between the two parties is
that the Liberals are generally in power and the Tories out.

This difference is both less obvious and more profound than it
first appears. The Liberals have been in office for forty-four of
the past fifty-five years, the Tories for only eleven. The result of
this lopsided imbalance has been that everybody, whether
Liberal or Tory, has come to consider the Liberals the natural
ruling party of the country. The Liberals think of the civil service, which is the crucial element in governing the country, as
their ally and soul-brother, while the Tories think of it as their
enemy. Conservatives are not only accustomed to being in opposition, but many of them have also come to like it. "The trouble
with the Conservative caucus," says one seasoned observer, "is
that most of them would rather be in opposition than in government. It's the same pay and half the responsibility."

The Tories' absolute lack of power also explains their tendency to dump their leaders. The Tories get rid of their leaders
because they lose elections. There was no dump-Diefenbaker

movement when he presided over two hundred and seven fellow Conservatives in the House of Commons. It is characteristic of parties in power that they handle their disputes swiftly and, to all appearances, decorously. What knives there are are wielded behind the arras. Dissatisfaction with the dominant thinking of the Liberal party drove John Turner to silence, Eric Kierans to academia and Paul Hellyer to the Toronto *Sun* and the Tory leadership race. Parties out of power have no such control over their dissidents.

Mother Earth in Autumn

In the press room after Stanfield's speech we hear a garbled announcement over the P.A. system. Members of the Alberta cabinet are going to clarify their position on the leadership race at an impromptu press conference. Alberta Attorney General Jim Foster and another cabinet minister, both wearing Clark buttons, are holding court in a small, steamy room at the back of the Civic Centre. They deny a statement that appeared in one of Brian Mulroney's handouts. The Mulroney statement seems innocuous enough, given the hyperbole of a leadership race: it is simply a claim that Mulroney has a lot of support in Alberta, and that his support will grow among members of the province's government from the second ballot on. Not so, say the Alberta cabinet ministers. The whole conference seems designed to show only that although the premier is sticking to his benign non-endorsement, Alberta officialdom in its majority is actively supporting Joe Clark.

Outside the Coliseum next to the Civic Centre, the Hoopla Gang is playing 'Deep in the Heart of Texas' as an overture to Mulroney's Ginette Reno concert inside. Ginette gives us ten songs at a thousand bucks apiece, and Brian sings 'When Irish Eyes are Smiling' to a crowd of two or three thousand. As at other Mulroney functions delegate badges are notable for their absence. We head for Flora's Hoedown downtown. On the way, one of us falls in with a delegate we had met a few times at pre-convention meetings.

"What did you think of Diefenbaker's speech last night?" he asks.

"What about Stanfield tonight?" we reply.

"I'd rather talk about Diefenbaker."

Flora's Hoedown is in the Commonwealth Ballroom of the Holiday Inn, and the attractions include a series of prizes, among them a watercolour donated by William Ronald and hamburgers

Flora MacDonald

donated by McDonald's. Special Grand Prize is dinner and maybe a swim with Flora MacDonald at 24 Sussex Drive — presumably this one will be donated by the taxpayers. Tickets for the raffle are a dollar.

John Allan Cameron has also donated his talent to the evening and there are pipers and square dancers, fiddlers and piano players. A group of young musicians, well amplified but otherwise unidentifiable, don't quite seem to fit — they are on first, and warm things up until Flora makes her entrance.

From eleven o'clock, the place is jammed. This of course is not unusual, everything is jammed. But unlike most of the other parties, Flora's is jammed not only with the thirsty, the curious and people attracted by the music but with genuine supporters — and there are plenty of delegate badges. In fact as the evening wears on, Flora's Hoedown has the aura not of an attention-getting device of the candidate, but rather of a tribute to her by her supporters and friends.

Flora, at this stage of the campaign, has become not a candidate but a cause.

We think back to the young lady in the bar the night before who found it so difficult to express her commitment to Flora. This has been the intangible quality of the Flora MacDonald campaign — and will be until it hits upon that very tangible thing called first-ballot votes.

Her initial base was the Ontario party and, if it hadn't been for the events of September 18, 1975, that might have been enough. But the Ontario election unbalanced a lot of the old power balances in the party. After the provincial Tories suffered their most serious losses in thirty years and were reduced to a minority, an endorsement from William Davis, explicit or otherwise, was worth about as much as one from Mao Tse-tung.

Eddie Goodman had begun collecting money for her but was not at the time supporting her, a distinction that seemed important to Fast Eddie. On the other hand he wasn't supporting anyone else either.

She was branded a Red Tory, a term that once had a precise meaning but by the end of the campaign was so debased that it was being used to describe Robert Stanfield; like most of the Red Tories, and to an even greater extent than Joe Clark, there was little in her positions to distinguish her from the mainstream Tories and even the right. She too wanted means tests for government assistance programs and decried the evils of government spending. She was branded one of Dalton Camp's candidates, having been an ally of Dalton's from the dump-Diefenbaker days of the 1960s, but she avoided being branded his first-string candidate, and quite happily saw that honour go to Mulroney instead.

She had, however, quite independently become the object of the undying animus of the Diefenbaker loyalists, and many of them saw her as second only to the devil incarnate in the form of Dalton Camp as an evil influence in the party. "Flora will round up all the free libs," said Dr. Jimmy Johnston, who as national director of the party in 1966 fired her from the national office, "all the left-wingers, all the kooks plus a lot of responsible people who don't know her. I know her very well and she's the bottom of anyone's heap."

Dr. Johnston, an amiable sort although something less than a genius as a political strategist, seems to have spent a large part of his time as national director playing practical jokes, often based on his faint physical resemblance to Camp, and thinking up puns. (His suggested slogan for Arthur Maloney's attempt to win the presidency from Camp in 1966 was 'Any way you slice it it's still Maloney.' It was not adopted.) He now publishes the Cobourg *Star* and several other small-town Ontario newspapers, maintains his friendship with John Diefenbaker, and votes Liberal so long as Dalton Camp is the power behind the scenes in the Conservative party.

The most congenial restaurant in Cobourg is, of all things, Marie Dressler's birthplace, maintained just the way it was when she lived there in the 1870s, and it was here that Dr. Johnston told us why he fired Flora MacDonald. "I'm proud to say I fired Flora," he said. "There were leaks from the national office and it was clear she was responsible for them. She was private secretary to the national director but she kept inventing titles for herself, and signed herself executive secretary. When Dick Thrasher was national director you could see the progression. First he would sign letters. Then it was Richard Thrasher per Flora MacDonald. Then it was 'Mr. Thrasher has asked me to reply to your letter.' Finally there was no reference to Thrasher at all — he probably didn't even know.

"She's a very unhappy, frustrated person. I had an insight into her character once flying low over Sydney. It's a barren place, and you had to scratch and claw there just to survive. She's been scratching and clawing all her life."

Dr. Johnston also explains Dalton Camp's character with references to his boyhood poverty in New Brunswick.

A few weeks after we talked to him he turned up as top man in the Ottawa office of the Paul Hellyer campaign. At the convention he could be seen leading bands of Hellyer musicians around.

Dr. Johnston's friend, John Diefenbaker, had a few unlikely
words of praise for Flora, paying tribute to the populist nature of
her campaign.

One can spend time talking about the Mulroney packaging
that took place during the campaign and convention, or the
amounts of money spent by the other candidates, but Flora Mac-
Donald was the most thoughtfully, artfully and slickly packaged
of them all. The folksiness of the campaign made the best use of
the candidate's personal qualities, which generated that fierce
loyalty to her among her supporters. She appealed to the women
of the country to support a candidate of their own sex by each
giving her a dollar, and in the latter stages of her campaign people at her meetings, women and men alike, regularly pulled dollar bills out of their pockets and pressed them into her hand.
There was something about Flora that made people want to give
her a dollar, if not to vote for her. She proudly proclaimed that
more people had donated money to her campaign than had
donated to the party as a whole in the previous year.

At the convention, she spent a lot of money to make herself
look poverty-stricken. People paid for the honour of getting up
early for cold toast and coffee at her breakfasts, her leaflets were
roughly mimeographed and crudely lettered, and when all the
other candidates organized elaborate luncheons in the hotels,
Flora took over a church basement and charged for home-made
soup and bread — lovely touches all. The unspoken motif of her
campaign was the simple life: organic food and the colours of
Mother Earth in autumn.

But for all that, it was a professional operation from beginning to end. With just plain folks like Toronto's Mayor Crombie
and New Brunswick's Premier Hatfield in tow and with a highly
sophisticated computer system locked away in the back room,
Flora made the classiest impression of the convention.

The crush around the bars is almost impassable, but after
finally getting our hands on a cold beer we push through the
overheated crowd upstairs to a balcony which overlooks the ballroom. On the stage the young singer, who has just launched himself on a ballad, answers the frantic waves of a harried individual
with a walkie-talkie and abruptly stops singing. After a few more
bars the rest of the musicians get the point and put away their
instruments.

Like magic, the crowd in the centre of the room parts to make
an aisle for the procession. First the cameraman stepping backward smartly, as if in step with the majestic piper who follows;
then comes Flora, looking as much like Sir John A. MacDonald

Heward Grafftey and CTV's Ann McMillan

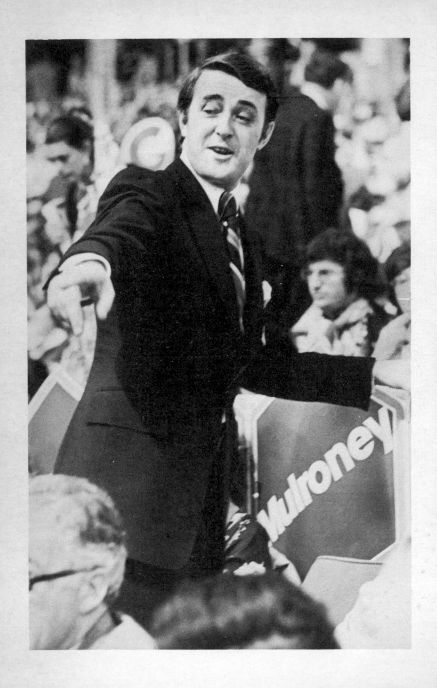

Kathy Davis, wife of the Ontario Premier, talks with Flora MacDonald

as one could reasonably expect of a 49-year-old woman. The crowd let out a good cheer and round of applause as she pushes in behind her entourage.

"Jesus," says a veteran of New Democratic Party wars, "it looks like the Waffle with its act together."

Flora is now on stage. She thanks everybody, says the usual things. Then she says that something is going on with her campaign, she can't express it, but there is movement and momentum. Everyone in the room understands what Flora is saying, they believe, like her, that things are moving and that maybe, just maybe, things may come together on Sunday.

As the evening wears on the crowd appears to grow. People are here now from the other parties around the city. There is lots of talk, lots of dancing, lots of drinking. Flora even gets a cheer from the crowd when she announces that the mother tongue of the majority of the Fathers of Confederation was Gaelic. A lot of people are even ready to drink to that now.

Flora leads the crowd around the stage in 'Alouette'. On her way out she dances a rather accomplished jig.

David Crombie, who seems to have worked hard for Flora throughout the convention, is still working the front of the hall, shaking every hand that passes. In the crowd we meet three delegates who have been travelling together throughout the convention and whom we have talked to several times before. They are still dithering between Hellyer and Horner.

"Well, what do you think about Flora?" we ask.

"See that God-dammed Mulroney," one of the men answers. "I just came from his joint — Ginette Reno — I used to run a club, I know she doesn't appear for less than seven thou . . . ."

"About Flora though," we persist.

"She's a fine woman," another answers. "But Flora MacDonald will never be leader of this party."

"We'll see you tomorrow."

"You bet."

Brian Mulroney

Interlude

The Hot Shot Lawyer and the Hanging Judge

In June, 1953, the world's attention was focussed on the coronation of Queen Elizabeth II, so even the keenest of observers might have been forgiven for failing to notice the beginning of the Quebec side of the Tory leadership race. It was on June 8 that three American hunters drove into the woods of the Gaspé Peninsula to hunt bear. They didn't drive out again.

The murdered bodies of Eugene Lindsay, his son Richard and Frederick Claar were found in late July. A local English-speaking prospector, Wilbert Coffin, had been the last person to see them alive, when their path crossed his on a remote trail. Coffin was picked up as a material witness, tried for murder, found guilty and sentenced to death. All appeal procedures failed, and Coffin was hanged in February, 1956.

That would have been that, had it not been for the widespread suspicion that Coffin was innocent, framed by the Duplessis régime, which was eager to solve a murder that was receiving widespread attention in the American press, and not doing the tourist trade any good at all.

Among those who said Coffin was framed was Sergeant Henri Doyon, the policeman originally assigned to the case. Doyon was pulled off the case when he persisted in looking for the real murderers, demoted, kicked off the force, and eventually incarcerated as a dangerous psychotic.

Another who cried fix was Jacques Hébert, the province's most prominent anti-Duplessis publisher, who wrote a book called *Coffin était innocent* in 1958, and followed it up with *J'accuse les assassins de Wilbert Coffin* in 1963. The assassins in question were the police, judges and politicians who had set Coffin up.

The first book provoked little reaction. The second, published almost three years after the Liberals under Jean Lesage had defeated the Union Nationale following the death of Duplessis,

created a storm of controversy. A Royal Commission was set up
to look into the matter. Looking after Hébert's interests before
the commission was his bosom chum, co-author of *Two Inno-
cents in Red China,* and colleague on the magazine *Cité libre,*
Pierre Elliott Trudeau.

The commission ruled that Hébert had not proven his case,
which meant that he had impugned the majesty of the legal system without just cause. The legal system was not slow to
respond. Hébert was sentenced to jail by a sessions court judge
for contempt of court, and spent three days inside before getting
out on appeal.

Joseph-Napoléon Claude Wagner was later to regret being the
judge who put Trudeau's best friend in the slammer.

In the summer of 1954, while Wilbert Coffin was still in jail
waiting to be hanged, Colonel Robert Rutherford McCormick,
owner of the Chicago *Tribune* and the New York *Daily News,*
decided to have a party at his country place in Baie-Comeau, the
town he'd founded by establishing the Quebec North Shore
Paper Co. mill there. To entertain his guests, he hired the son of
an electrician in the plant, a boy who was said to have a pretty
good voice. Brian Mulroney sang 'Dearie', and picked up fifty
bucks for his trouble, not bad for a fourteen-year-old who normally worked as a labourer in the summer, to help pay for his
high-school education in Chatham, N.B.

It was a long road from 'Dearie' in Col. McCormick's hunting
lodge to 'When Irish Eyes Are Smiling' in the Coliseum next to
the Ottawa Civic Arena, but charm and hard work go a long
way, even for a working-class kid from Baie-Comeau.

Mulroney went from Chatham to St. Francis Xavier University in Antigonish, N.S. and it was there that he joined the Progressive Conservative party, mostly because it was the social thing
to do. He voted for Diefenbaker at the 1956 convention. He
picked up a law degree at Laval University in Quebec City,
graduating in 1963, and moved to Montreal, joining the firm of
Ogilvy, Cope, Porteous and specializing in labour relations as a
management representative.

Mulroney teamed up with three other young Tories, Egan
Chambers, Brian Gallery and Michael Meighen, and began a
mission to bring Quebec English Torydom out of the wilderness.
It's still in the wilderness, but no one can say the Westmount
Four didn't try. They assiduously called meetings, and chartered
buses which rode almost empty to the meeting halls. They held
countless press events to which no press came.

They were candidates and organizers in search of a constituency. Egan Chambers was elected in the 1958 Diefenbaker
sweep, but served only one term, losing in 1962 to a young
Liberal comer named John Turner. Meighen was a perennial losing PC candidate against Bud Drury in Westmount. Gallery and
Mulroney organized away, trying to forge a constituency out of
the young, conservative, federalist-but-still-Quebec-nationalist
forces, a difficult bunch to find.

They thought that this rather closely-defined constituency
could be found in the remains of the Union Nationale, and in
1971, they worked on the campaign of Marcel Masse for the UN
leadership, believing Masse to be the only man who could revive
Duplessis's old party. As delegates to the UN convention in
June, they were able to watch their man get beaten by Gabriel
Loubier, a wealthy lawyer who had served as Minister of Tour-
ism, Fish and Game under Premiers Daniel Johnson and Jean-
Jacques Bertrand.

As they went into the 1976 Tory convention, the Westmount
Four were still organizing, but not all in the same direction.
Brian Gallery, who had finally been elected to something (the
Westmount City Council, in late 1975), had joined the Mulroney
bandwagon a couple of weeks before, having finally given up
being the head of the Quebec Draft Lougheed movement.
Michael Meighen had got himself elected national president of
the party, and was therefore above it all (though tilting Mulron-
eywards). Egan Chambers was Flora MacDonald's Quebec
Chairman. Mulroney was The Candidate.

Chambers' wife, incidentally, is Gretta Chambers, who
reviewed the press coverage of the convention for CBC's Capital
Report the next week, and who is the sister of Charles Taylor,
formerly the NDP's Great White Hope for Quebec. One of Taylor's campaign workers in Mount Royal riding in 1963 was his
university colleague Pierre Elliott Trudeau, who later became a
Liberal and ran against and defeated Taylor in the same riding
in 1965.

Mulroney's career as a labour lawyer was rather more successful than his career as a party organizer and candidate. As the
labour specialist in Montreal's largest law firm, always acting for
the management side, he racked up an impressive series of
successes. One of the more spectacular cases was the *La Presse*
strike, which began with a lockout in July 1971, and developed
into a conflict that involved the whole Quebec labour movement.
In the spring of 1972, acting for the newspaper's owners, Power

Corporation, Mulroney achieved a settlement in 48 hours. He is regarded by all on the labour side as honest and straightforward: when the unions have to deal with a boss's lawyer, they like to deal with a straight-shooter like Mulroney. It is a very different picture from Mulroney the candidate.

Stories about Claude Wagner's childhood are somehow reminiscent of Nixon stories. "He was the little boy whose pants were always pressed," say people who grew up with him. As was said of Nixon, a perfect Christmas present would have been a nice shiny new briefcase.

He was the sort of boy you would predict would grow up to become a judge.

Wagner practised law in Montreal (for part of the time at the firm where Robert Lemieux, the FLQ lawyer, later worked) from 1949 to 1960, when the new Lesage administration appointed him Crown prosecutor. He prosecuted *Lady Chatterley's Lover;* Georges Marcotte, the bank robber who machine-gunned two policemen to death while wearing a Santa Claus suit; the Georges Lemay gang for a $500,000 bank job pulled off with a tunnel; gambling joints long tolerated under Duplessis; and corrupt officials, including a Liberal caught on the take. They were all headline cases.

He got even more headlines after he was named a Sessions Court Judge in 1963 — at 38, the youngest in the province's history. The bench became something of a pulpit, from which law-and-order sermons were preached. Criminals were a bunch of cowards, murderers and bandits who had been pampered too long. Hanging was too good for them. In one of his first cases, he sentenced a man to ten years for a hold-up that netted $1.90.

But he really made his name with the celebrated "Meunier Affair", in which he busted a fellow judge — Adrien Meunier of the Superior Court, who was also a former Liberal MP.

And he sentenced Jacques Hébert for contempt.

In 1964, Premier Lesage gave the prominent law-and-order judge a call. Would he like to run in a by-election in Verdun, and be Solicitor-General? Yes, he would.

Wagner entered the cabinet in August, and one of his first assignments was to co-ordinate all the security arrangements for the Queen's October visit to Quebec City. The visit provoked one of the first big separatist-leftist demonstrations of the sixties, and the police went berserk. Journalists, passersby and spectators were clubbed along with demonstrators, and the event became known as *Le samedi de la matraque* — Nightstick Saturday. A week later, Wagner endorsed an internal inquiry to the effect that dangerous subversives had caused the whole thing, and that the police had acted properly. He was rewarded for his commitment to even-handed justice with a promotion to Attorney-General on October 31.

"When I think," he reflected, "of what I see elsewhere, in South America, where the nightsticks are longer than ours . . ." And later, "No, Quebec doesn't have the best [judicial] system in the world, but it's close to the best."

The crew-cut Attorney-General became Canada's first provincial Justice Minister in June, 1965.

If his childhood resembled Richard Nixon's, his ministerial style was like Joe McCarthy's.

He was constantly waving files in public, files he said contained the names of organized crime kingpins, incontrovertible proof of an all-powerful underworld, a "parallel power" of untouchables who were strangling Quebec. He would engage these chieftains of crime in a fight to the death, "and work to instill in our province a new conception of justice."

The files were waved at every opportunity, but never, not once, was a single name revealed or a single organized criminal prosecuted. The files he was constantly waving were empty.

In June 1966, the Union Nationale made a surprise comeback under Daniel Johnson, and Wagner was relegated to the back benches. Since the back benches furnished less limelight than The Bench, he petitioned the federal Liberals for a judgeship. No dice. The Hon. member for Verdun faded from the front page, except for a brief reappearance in 1967, when he exposed a scandal of underworld involvement at Expo 67. The scandal was there all right, but Wagner got the names, companies and contracts all wrong, and implicated a lot of innocent people.

By May 1969 Wagner had had enough of obscurity. He opened his campaign for the Quebec Liberal leadership, quite undeterred by the fact that the party had a leader, Jean Lesage, who had every intention of contesting another election. Wagner agitated for a leadership convention, splitting the party. Lesage resigned when the support he was counting on from Ottawa failed to come through.

Wagner's behaviour was of the sort that Liberals consider pushy, vulgar and typical of Tories. He had sealed his own doom. Wagner once said, "I'm like Joan of Arc. I hear voices." If he had been listening carefully, he could have heard them saying: "You're like Joan of Arc in more ways than one. You're going to be burnt at the stake."

Every political observer of acumen in Quebec will tell you that if the January, 1970, Liberal leadership had been fair, Claude Wagner would now be the Premier of the province. He played all his trumps during the campaign, as the Justice Minister of the People who had waged tireless (if fruitless) war on the crime bosses, had not shirked from his duty of clapping the influential in irons, and had taken a firm line with dangerous long-haired revolutionaries.

He went into the convention with a clear majority of the delegates elected by the riding associations. He had it sewn up.

But Wagner had just too many raps against him. Power in Ottawa was in the hands of Pierre Trudeau, Jean Marchand and Gérard Pelletier, the "three wise men", veterans of the anti-Duplessis movement. They didn't want Jean Lesage as Quebec Liberal leader, but they didn't want Claude Wagner either. In 1965, Pelletier, then still a journalist, had written an open letter to Wagner, likening him to Duplessis and his equally corrupt predecessor, Taschereau, denouncing him as a prejudiced, hidebound conservative who demonstrated, with disconcerting enthusiasm, the limits of his own horizons. He would hardly have been the candidate for the enlightened troika up in Ottawa — even if he hadn't put Trudeau's best friend in jail.

The fixers were Trudeau, his Quebec lieutenant Marchand, and the very disgruntled Lesage. Their chosen instrument was the virtually unknown Liberal finance critic in the National Assembly, an accountant who married money, Robert Bourassa. The tools for the job were 1,000 *ex officio* delegates appointed by the party establishment.

When Bourassa took the Quebec City convention, Wagner was apoplectic. With his wife Gisèle, a tough lady with some very sharp corners indeed, tugging on his arm and urging him to go home, he had to be physically pushed up onto the stage to accept his defeat at the hands of Bourassa, Lesage and the federal Liberals.

The Best Candidate Money Can Buy

Meanwhile, back in the wilderness, Mulroney was watching these developments with a degree of interest. After all, he and the rest of the Westmount Four were not only candidates in search of a constituency, they were a constituency in search of a Tory candidate in Quebec. One who could win for once.

Wagner came out of the Liberal convention without the leadership, but with his popularity intact. He still looked like a win-

ner, someone who could deliver a lot of votes. And the Westmount Four weren't the only people thinking that way.

Trudeau and Bourassa tried desperately to woo Wagner back
into the Liberal fold, but it wasn't to be. He quit the party. The
Union Nationale premier, Jean-Jacques Bertrand, appointed him
back to the bench, putting him on ice for a while and establishing a debt that might come in handy should Wagner re-enter
politics.

The appointment was made on the same day that Bertrand
announced the election in which his party was all but wiped out.

Wagner sat out the Bourassa landslide election and the October Crisis.

He was widely touted as a man with a political future and
whenever there was a party in search of a leader, his name would
crop up. Meetings were held with the devastated Union Nationale and the Créditistes, but no satisfactory deal could be struck.
It was in September, 1971, that the federal Tories joined the
Wagner hunt in earnest.

The story of how Wagner became a Tory in 1972 is crucial to
understanding Joe Clark's convention, but even more crucial is
the way in which the story was revealed in the Toronto press in
1975 and 1976.

The key newspaper articles are known in Tory circles as *Manthorpe I, Manthorpe II,* and *White-Mackenzie.*

Manthorpe I appeared in the *Globe and Mail* on November 4,
1975, under the bylines of Jonathan Manthorpe and Hugh Win-
sor.

In it, Wagner acknowledged for the first time that his conversion to Torydom had resulted in the setting up of the famous
trust fund, which gave him an income in addition to his salary as
an MP. *Manthorpe I* confirmed that the fund contained $300,000
and gave Wagner an income of $30,000 a year before taxes. It
recalled Wagner's statement when, having resigned from the
bench, he announced his candidacy in St-Hyacinthe riding on
September 5, 1972: "I have no need of, I have not asked for, nor
have I been offered any pension fund or financial compensation."

Wagner told the *Globe* that there was no inconsistency here,
because the fund had not been set up until *after* the October,
1972, election.

Manthorpe I was hardly a scoop, since the trust fund story
had been appearing on and off in the Quebec papers since early
1972. It was first written by Claude Arpin, of the Montreal *Star,*
who cited his source as two Quebec City lawyers. Arpin's article
said that negotiations were going on between Wagner and the

federal Tories, and mentioned $400,000 as the amount of the financial guarantee being asked.

Financial help for politicians is nothing new, as the Tories were quick to point out. Louis St-Laurent and Lester Pearson were both given a few bucks to tide them over those difficult years in public life.

There is also an amusing story about the late Marcel Faribault, Wagner's predecessor as the Tories' putative Great White Hope for Quebec. Faribault went to see Prime Minister Diefenbaker, and announced that he would be quite happy to help out — if he could have External Affairs, the Deputy Prime Ministership, and half a million dollars. Dief threw him out of his office. About a week later, Faribault went to see Dief again, and said he had reconsidered. Under the circumstances, and interest rates being what they were, he thought he could manage it for External Affairs, Deputy PM, and a mere $300,000. He got the door again. Some years later, however, he did become Robert Stanfield's Quebec lieutenant, but was unable to win a seat.

Manthorpe II hit the streets on January 10, 1976. It had a splendid scene-setter lead: "It was late in the afternoon of September 10, 1971, and the evening gloom came early to the second floor apartment in an old house in Westmount. The failing light enriched the always dark apartment, making more sumptuous the colours of the velvet draperies, the classic stripes of the upholstery and the solid furniture.

"There were three men in the apartment. The host was Brian Mulroney, a young lawyer with everything going for him . . ."

The other two men were Robert Stanfield and Claude Wagner.

The Tories were expecting an election to be called the next year, and Mulroney had been asked to find someone in Quebec who could be Stanfield's George Etienne Cartier (the man who took care of French Canada for Sir John A.). Mulroney's attention had been drawn to Wagner by Peter White, publisher of the Sherbrooke *Record.* Mulroney set up the dinner with Stanfield, who was impressed with Wagner, and hinted that he might be in line for the leadership when Stanfield decided to quit.

There was nó talk of money at the meeting, which was also attended briefly by Premier Richard Hatfield of New Brunswick (who later ended up supporting Flora MacDonald).

Manthorpe II went on to tell about further chats between Mulroney and Wagner, in which the judge brought up the question of "security", and underlined Mulroney's adamant denial that anything more specific — such as, for example, several hundred thousand dollars — was ever mentioned. Mulroney maintained he passed on the security question to Stanfield and the party's campaign committee chairman, Finlay MacDonald. Manthorpe quoted "people who were on the fringes of what was going on" as saying that at this time, MacDonald made a counter-offer to Wagner of $150,000 plus a guaranteed place in a Montreal law firm, which Mulroney tried to arrange in early 1972.

Wagner was understandably worried about his future. Tories had a habit of being defeated in Quebec. There wasn't going to be any Jean-Jacques Bertrand around to give him another judgeship, and he certainly wasn't going to get anything out of his former Liberal colleagues. A guaranteed spot in a law firm might have filled the bill. Unfortunately, Mulroney was unable to find anyone who wanted to have Wagner as a partner, so it was back to square one.

In February, 1972, the Tories commissioned Robert Teeter of Market Opinion Research in Detroit to conduct a poll in Quebec, hoping to find out who could lead them out of the wilderness. They composed questions about Wagner, Marcel Masse (the Westmount Four's candidate for the Union Nationale leadership), and, as controls, other popular Quebec figures such as Jean Drapeau and Pierre Trudeau.

Wagner came out on top, and the Tories renewed their efforts to snare him. They didn't realize at the time that something was wrong with the Teeter poll. The Detroit sage, with his wide knowledge of Quebec, had forgotten to mention in his questionnaire that Wagner would be running as a Tory with the Liberals screaming "turncoat" at every opportunity.

In April, according to Manthorpe, Mulroney bowed out of the picture, leaving for Europe and a holiday with his friend Michel Cogger. He was called back to work suddenly, and spent June and July working on a labour dispute for a major client. He spent the rest of the summer playing tennis and chasing his future wife.

The Wagner ball was now in the hands of Finlay MacDonald and Eddie Goodman, the Toronto lawyer and party bagman (who was Flora's bagperson in the leadership race).

Goodman and Finlay MacDonald held a meeting with Wagner in the second week of July. In September Wagner declared his candidacy and issued the trust-fund denial.

Manthorpe II ended by leaving the key question — the date on which the George Etienne Cartier Trust, as it became known, was set up — "locked in the memories of four people who refuse to discuss the matter." The four were Finlay MacDonald, who lives in Florida, Goodman, who claims lawyer-client privilege, Wagner, and his wife Gisèle.

That, then, was the substance of *Manthorpe II*, except for paragraph 69.

Robert Mackenzie, the Toronto *Star's* Quebec City correspondent, wasn't the only person to notice paragraph 69, but he was the one who found himself in a position to do something about it.

He happened to be having dinner with Peter White not long after *Manthorpe II* came out, and during the course of conversation, he happened to mention the oddity of paragraph 69. It read:

"Before election day, Mr. Wagner received the first payment on the fund. It was delivered by hand on Oct. 26 to Mr. Wagner's home and was accepted by Mrs. Wagner."

If this was true, it meant that Wagner had been lying when he said that the fund was set up *after* the election. Unaware that White was the source for most of *Manthorpe II,* Mackenzie pointed out the strangeness of leading an article with sumptuous velvet in the gloom of a Westmount evening and burying what any journalism student would recognize as the real lead in the sixty-ninth paragraph. He allowed as how he wouldn't mind rewriting the story with the lead in the proper place. White hinted that he might be able to help.

Realizing that White knew more than he was telling, Mackenzie began pursuing him. A couple of weeks later, the two kept an appointment in Mulroney's Montreal campaign HQ. They chatted briefly with Cogger, then went to the restaurant downstairs, where White laid it all out.

White-Mackenzie appeared in the Toronto *Star* on February 7, 1976 (twelve days before the convention), under the headline "Wagner given cash before '72 election former aide says." There was no sumptuous velvet in the lead: "A large sum in cash was delivered in a briefcase to the Montreal home of Tory leadership candidate Claude Wagner four days before the 1972 federal election, a former close associate says."

White-Mackenzie also made much more of a story that *Manthorpe II* glossed over in paragraph 68. White was an aide to Wagner during the 1972 campaign. He said that he received a phone call from Goodman in Wagner's suite in the Queen Elizabeth hotel during the campaign. He said Goodman asked him if he would be a trustee of a fund that was being set up for Wagner. He refused, and passed the phone to Wagner, who had been in the room throughout.

In early editions, the *Star* also printed a letter from White to Wagner advising against a leadership bid because of an "obvious ethical problem" over the fund.

White denied Wagner's claim that the fund was to finance his activities as Quebec leader, and said he urged Wagner to "get out" of the fund after he was elected because he no longer needed it, now that he had an MP's salary.

Having chosen, at the time of *Manthorpe I,* to take what Nixon aides called the modified limited hangout route, Wagner stonewalled throughout the rest of the campaign. *White-Mackenzie* was the last of the revelations. Meanwhile, the articles were having their effect behind the scenes, and ended up doing Wagner, the target, more good than harm, and Mulroney, whose people leaked the information, more harm than good.

Jean-Yves Lortie has an incredibly vulgar silver punch bowl with a little pump in it. It's a three-tier affair, topped by a cherub taking a leak. When Jean-Yves wants to impress a gathering, he brings out his punch bowl and fills it up with Pernod and orange juice. This rather quaint mixture runs through the pump up to the cherub, who pisses it out over the three tiers to create a golden fountain effect. Jean-Yves Lortie is the Secretary-General of the Quebec Progressive Conservative Association. The punch bowl and the strong arm are his principal campaign tools.

Whenever the punch bowl shows up at a convention you can be sure that Lortie is the man behind the men behind the guy who is trying to get elected to something. The punch bowl was very much in evidence when Claude Dupras became the President of the Quebec Progressive Conservative Party Association, and again when Michael Meighen became PC national president.

Lortie knows what he's doing. But it was Claude Dupras who was running the Tory effort in Quebec during the 1972 election.

Wagner had already changed from a crew cut to a JFK cut at the time of his Liberal leadership bid. Dupras decided that his brand-new Quebec Tory leader needed to soften his image even more. The rigid law-and-order crimebuster was put into a turtleneck sweater and sent off round the province preaching justice tempered with humanity and moderation. Ironically, it was in

Baie-Comeau that Wagner came to his senses, called the whole thing off and rushed back to his home riding, St-Hyacinthe, where he was in deep trouble.

His opponents were Liberal Paul Foster, whose campaign was being managed by Paul Desrochers, Bourassa's eminence grise who had looked after the nuts and bolts of rigging the Liberal leadership convention, and Martha Adams, the province's most celebrated Madam.

Martha wasn't causing much trouble, but you couldn't walk the streets of St-Hyacinthe without falling over a cabinet minister or even Margaret Trudeau come to give Desrochers a hand.

Another problem was a slim volume called *Le Dossier Wagner.* It was written by civil-liberties lawyer Claude-Armand Sheppard (who later defended abortionist Henry Morgentaler). Sheppard felt it his duty as a citizen during the election campaign to write one of the most devastating hatchet jobs ever perpetrated by one member of the legal profession on another. It was published by Les Editions du Jour, Jacques Hébert's publishing house. The book mentioned the trust fund in passing, but concentrated on describing what was wrong with Wagner from a lawyer's point of view. It certainly didn't help the Wagner effort.

It is a measure of the popularity of the book that more than three years after publication, Joe Clark's Quebec campaign had quite a number of copies on hand, one of which was offered to us to help in our pre-convention research.

Things looked pretty desperate when Wagner, Peter White, and the rest of the team got back from the campaign trail to try to salvage the new leader's home riding.

It seems clear that at this stage the trust fund had been agreed on and promised, but was still in the process of being set up by Goodman, his law partner Lionel Schipper and yet another lawyer and party bagman, Patrick Vernon. With Wagner facing possible defeat, a guarantee of good faith was definitely in order.

Manthorpe II described the secret of the fund as "locked in the memories of four people who refuse to discuss the matter." One of those four has confirmed, off the record of course, that on October 26, four days before the election, a messenger rang the doorbell of the Wagner home, carrying a suitcase.

Gisèle Wagner answered, and according to another source, took the suitcase down to the basement playroom and counted the $20,000 in cash it contained before the messenger left.

As Peter White, who was working for Wagner at the time, told Manthorpe and Mackenzie, the money came from Goodman's office. That too has been confirmed off the record by one of the four with the locked memories.

Normal campaign funds from the national party to ridings in Quebec are sent to Montreal, and from there to the individual campaigns, by cheque.

The $20,000 in the suitcase was an advance guarantee of good faith that the trust fund was indeed coming.

Wagner, it seems, was telling the truth when he gave his modified limited hang-out route statement that the fund was set up after the election, but not on September 5, 1972, when he said "I have no need of, I have not asked for, nor have I been offered any pension fund or financial compensation". The details of the fund were agreed to at the meeting of Goodman, Finlay MacDonald and Wagner at a Montreal hotel on July 10. A solemn bargain was struck, but the actual constituting of the fund took place later.

Goodman, MacDonald and Wagner were not the only people at the July meeting. There was a fourth man, a young Montreal lawyer with everything going for him.

Contrary to his denials of any knowledge of what, if any, "security" arrangements were made for Wagner, and despite his pious promise to hold an inquiry into the circumstances surrounding the trust, Brian Mulroney took time off from his labour negotiations to attend the very meeting at which the deal was struck. He was happy afterwards to assure party bigwigs of the uncontroversial nature of the trust, secure in the knowledge that the papers wouldn't be signed until after the election.

There's also every reason to believe that he was the original source of the rumour that Claude Arpin picked up from two Quebec City lawyers. Mulroney is said to have complained that Wagner was asking too much — hence the $400,000 figure in the original story about the fund.

In defence of the Tories, it's only fair to note that the Liberals bought themselves two Prime Ministers (St-Laurent and Pearson), while the Tories only got a pig in a poke, who managed to reduce the party's Quebec representation by fifty per cent — from four to two, one of whom, Heward Grafftey, had neglected to bring his party affiliation to the attention of the voters.

Where did the $300,000 for the fund come from? Wagner says he thought it was from unknown admirers, "friends", but admits that it could have come from party funds, even though he was assured that it didn't. It did.

National HQ originally budgeted $1,400,000 for the Quebec wing in the 1972 election, but suddenly cut that back to a million after the July meeting. Nobody can remember what happened to the odd $80,000 left over after the suitcase and the trust.

Honest Bob Stanfield knew all about the George Etienne Cartier Trust too. Those who were organizing it kept him in touch, but built in a good deniability factor. He didn't attend any key meetings after the sumptuous velvet one in *Manthorpe II* but was briefed on developments. Stanfield did say when asked about it that he wouldn't be surprised if some arrangements had been made for Wagner's security.

With a Little Help from Their Friends

After the 1972 débâcle, Jean-Yves Lortie got out his punch bowl and went on the road. Having the common touch in abundance, Lortie realized that you don't get anywhere in Quebec by concentrating on the top; the only way to do it is through grassroots organization.

Lortie said, "I ran Dupras. I ran Meighen. Now I want to run a Prime Minister." Claude Wagner was his choice, and he came pretty close to making it.

The silver cherub pissed away gallons of Pernod and orange juice from one end of the province to the other, and by the time it was over, Lortie had more than doubled the number of functioning riding associations, bringing it up to the full complement of 74. He also saw to it that the grassroots he was watering so abundantly were all of strong Wagner stock.

It looked as though Jean-Yves had it sewn up for Wagner. Until August, 1975, it was clear to almost everyone that Wagner was going to show up at the convention with at least 600 of the 639 Quebec delegates. Heward Grafftey had declared in July, but nobody was taking him seriously. Although Wagner still hadn't declared, it was in August that he signed up a helper to go with his JFK haircut — Rich Willis, a shrewd political gun for hire who had been one of Bobby Kennedy's principal organizers. It was also in August that Brian Mulroney decided to move.

Mulroney had a very high profile in Quebec since his appointment in 1974 to the Cliche Commission into violence in the construction industry. Many people thought he had it all going for him, and persuaded him to seek the leadership.

One can understand the chagrin that this caused in the Wagner camp, not least because it was Mulroney who had brought Wagner into the party in the first place.

As the riding association meetings to choose delegates unfolded in late fall, there were some pretty murky goings-on as the Mulroney and Wagner machines struggled for control.

On the Mulroney side were a section of the party organization

led by Provincial President Claude Dupras, the business community, and a gang of lawyers. The Wagner side consisted of Jean-
Yves Lortie, Rich Willis, and the rump of the Union Nationale.
Aside from Mulroney's business and legal support, it was his
young federalist nationalist conservatives against Wagner's old
nationalist federalist conservatives. Experience won out.

Jean-Yves Lortie managed to dredge up some pretty strange
Tories. In one Montreal riding, the nominating meeting was held
in a bar. The Mulroney and Clark forces had worked out a slate
that gave them three delegates each. It looked pretty good until
the local motorcycle gang, card-carrying party members to a
man, elected the Wagner slate. A senior citizens' club, all sudden
converts to the Tory cause, is said to have voted in at least two
ridings. One of those meetings was held at eleven in the morning, a time designed to encourage the elderly vote. Another nominating meeting was held at 2 pm on Grey Cup Day.

Mulroney's boys were trying, but after fifteen meetings they
were up against the ropes. They blew the whistle, and Robert
Stanfield stepped in, a special surveillance committee was
worked out, and some meetings were held again. The meeting
that had been held at 11 am was rescheduled for 7 pm on Christmas Eve.

Under the circumstances, Mulroney didn't do badly at all. It
is estimated that Wagner showed up at the convention with
about 400 Quebec delegates, Mulroney about 175, enough to
stop the Wagner strategy of steamrolling the convention. The
only other candidate who got anywhere was Joe Clark, who had
the remaining fifty or so.

The Clark campaign in Quebec was chaired by Jean-Gaston
Rivard, a former Royal Canadian Navy pay officer who is now a
chiropractor. He and his organization put on a strong performance, and Clark worked the province hard, including going
door-to-door during the Hochelaga byelection in mid-November.
Tories speak about Hochelaga the way Churchill did about the
Battle of Britain. A local candidate, radiology technician Jacques
Lavoie, beat the Liberal parachutist, Pierre Juneau, and ended
his brief career as federal Communications Minister.

The Hochelaga effort was led by Roch Lasalle, the MP for
Joliette who announced his intention not to run again as a Tory
when Wagner was defeated by Clark. It is rumoured that he will
join the Union Nationale with an arrangement similar to the one
Wagner has with the Tories, except with a smaller amount of
money. Behind the scenes in Hochelaga was Jean-Yves Lortie,
his punch bowl, and the remnants of the Union Nationale
machine.

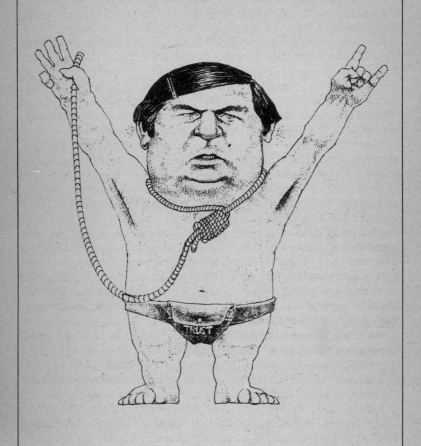

Claude Wagner

When Flora MacDonald finally showed up in Quebec, the party HQ wouldn't even give her a list of delegates.

The fight over the sandbagging of the nominating meetings was loud enough, but mild compared with the rumpus caused by the selection of the delegates-at-large. Sixteen of the thirty-seven delegates were chosen by women's and youth organizations. The other twenty-one were elected by the provincial council. Among those rejected by the Wagner-controlled council were Brian Mulroney, his campaign manager, Michel Cogger, Mulroney's law partner (and party bagman) Jack Porteous, Liam O'Brian (a former national director of the party and one of Mulroney's gang of lawyers), and Jacques Courtois (bagman, Mulroneyite, and president of the Montreal Canadiens hockey team).

One of the delegate seats left open by eliminating all the prominent tories who supported Mulroney went to Wagner's son Richard, who attends the University of Ottawa and had been axed as a delegate by Mulroney forces there.

Meanwhile, similar shenanigans were going on in Ontario, where Alan Eagleson (provincial party president, president of the National Hockey League Players' Association and Mulroney supporter) contrived to deny a delegate seat to Douglas Bassett, who was thought to be tilting towards Wagner. That proved to be a major mistake. Bassett is John Bassett's son and a business-man and newspaper owner in his own right. His string of local Ontario papers ran their first editorial against the province's Tory government in their history.

At about Christmastime Wagner was broke. Most of the peo-ple who would normally have given him money were withhold-ing it because of his stonewalling on the trust fund. *Manthorpe I* had already appeared, but there were still outstanding questions. Potential Wagner backers were holding back.

Contrary to the suspicion of Mulroney's Ontario backers, Doug Bassett doesn't seem to have been a Wagner supporter until after he was bumped from the delegation. He was a mem-ber of a group known as The Common Front, ironically named after the Quebec union consortium. The other two members of the Front were Fred Eaton of the department-store family and Conrad Black, Peter White's partner in Sterling newspapers, a chain of eight dailies and weeklies. The Common Front, which welded three influential people into a power bloc, had not, as far as is known, made any move before early January.

The Common Front was apparently biding its time, holding back support until the most propitious moment and candidate appeared. They certainly were potential Wagner backers, but were unlikely to make a move while the trust fund was still up in the air. Alan Eagleson seems to have changed all that. Almost the same day that Bassett was denied a delegate spot, people started getting phone calls, asking them for money for Wagner.

After the appearance of *Manthorpe II*, the Common Front moved into high gear. It was generally thought that the article cleared the whole fund thing up. More phone calls were made, and personal cheques were written. Bassett is said to have given ten thousand, his father five, while Black is rumoured to have contributed as much as fifteen thousand.

Wagner spent about $120,000 on his leadership bid, with perhaps about 70 per cent of that raised by the Common Front after Bassett was dumped and *Manthorpe II* appeared. Without that $80,000 or so, there would have been no Wagner delegates at the convention, no band, no white hats, and no motel rooms in Hull paid for. Wagner would have been out of the running.

This theory may be confirmed by an incident one of us spotted after Wagner's Saturday speech. Coming off the stage, Wagner hugged Conrad Black, and Gisèle gave him a peck on the cheek. Gisèle is not an especially warm person, and one can presume that Black is held in very special esteem in the Wagner household.

While Wagner was having money problems, Mulroney was riding high. He not only had the services of senior party bagmen such as Jacques Courtois and Jack Porteous, but he had the backing of the business community, numbering a raft of major firms among his clients. The one that irked the other candidates the most, and caused much adverse publicity, was Power Corporation, the giant whose attempt to take over fellow giant Argus Corporation led to the appointment of the Bryce Commission on Corporate Concentration. Mulroney had solved the bitter *La Presse* strike for Power, and when the time came, Power returned the favour.

In December and January, everybody was eager to tell us how Mulroney was flying around the country in a Power Corp. jet. We heard it from both Dalton Camp and Sean O'Sullivan, who don't agree on anything else. They were wrong, but the real plane story is much more interesting.

At one point in the campaign, Mulroney, had to get to Winnipeg in a hurry and there were no convenient commercial flights. He leased a DH125 used by Eaton's and Domtar (an Argus subsidiary) — it is common practice for companies to share time on a plane, and lease it out when they don't need it.

Mulroney was dead from the minute he stepped into that

plane. Somebody who was there said, "He was a kid with a new toy. After that first flight, you couldn't get him out of the damn thing." Stricken with campaign fever, Mulroney scrapped his original strategy of laying back and entering the convention as a dark horse, and decided to try to become a front-runner. He made himself vulnerable, and opened the way for Joe Clark.

What Power Corp. did do for Mulroney was give him $10,000. They gave similar amounts to Wagner and MacDonald and $3,000 to Grafftey. Wagner and Grafftey had to go in person to Paul Desmarais's office to pick up their cheques.

Power also supplied some salaried staff to help out, but the most important thing they did was what The Common Front did for Wagner — they made phone calls. Calls from Paul or Louis Desmarais carried a lot of clout, and raised money almost as fast as Mulroney was spending it.

Another corporate helper, according to some sources, was the Royal Bank, which is closely linked to Power Corp. Apparently local Mulroney committees frequently had as a member and adviser the local manager of the Royal Bank.

Even this kind of help wasn't quite enough. Two weeks before the convention the campaign had spent $300,000, and the chief fund-raiser, David Angus, was getting flak from campaign manager Michel Cogger because they were running a deficit. Angus renewed his efforts. All along, he told prospective contributors that there was no need to worry about being named, because Mulroney was going to ignore the party rule about disclosure of funds.

The Mulroney organization contained an odd collection of people, and strangest of all perhaps was Peter White. He experienced a dramatic conversion from being a long-time Wagner worker. His major contribution to the Mulroney campaign was acting as the source for *White-Mackenzie,* which was widely interpreted as a smear against Wagner deliberately leaked by the Mulroney campaign in a moment of panic at seeing Wagner ahead. The effort to hamper Wagner with adverse publicity backfired badly, as Mulroney reaped a reputation for being a dirty trickster.

White spent the convention at the Embassy Hotel, which was Mulroney HQ, against Cogger's wishes. As a compromise solution to keep him away from the press, he was registered in his wife's name. Mary White supported Clark.

White's other contribution was to hire a staff for the Mulroney daily convention paper. He chose two pillars of the Montreal press corps: a sports reporter from Canadian Press and a police reporter from the Montreal *Star.* The latter immediately told his colleague Claude Arpin that the Mulroney paper would be printing the full, gory details of the trust fund. This was repeated in the *Star*, further adding to Mulroney's dirty-tricks image; the trust fund story was not written for the Mulroney paper; and the two reporters were not paid for their work.

Some youth delegates from the west also ended up with the dirty end of the stick financially. On Sunday night they didn't get the room money they'd been promised. About four hundred delegate rooms were paid for by the Mulroney campaign, rather more than his number of first-ballot votes.

White alone was strange enough, but the Mulroney ranks were also swelled by Richard B. Holden and Robert Y. MacGregor. Holden, who prosecuted Consumer Affairs Minister André Ouellet for contempt of court, later launched what became 'the Affair of the Judges' by leaking letters written by his former law partner Judge Kenneth Mackay, who complained to Justice Minister Ron Basford that Holden hadn't been paid, and threw in a few allegations of ministerial hanky-panky.

Holden's client, MacGregor, owns a travel agency called MacGregor Travel, whose questionable dealings with Air Canada were exposed by Elmer MacKay, who nominated Wagner at the convention.

Another element in the faintly grubby aura that surrounded the Mulroney campaign was its apparent involvement with the bizarre leadership bid of Joseph Zappia.

Zappia, who was disqualified as a candidate at the same time as Leonard Jones, got the boot because of irregularities in his nominating papers. It turned out that twenty-six of the fifty signatures on the papers duplicated those on Mulroney's list.

Zappia is a prominent construction contractor in Montreal. He controls the consortium whose no-tender contracts to build the Olympic village have been regarded by most observers as the next best thing to a licence to print money. The consortium, Terrasses Zarolega, is under RCMP investigation. Zappia's candidacy and its unsavoury dénouement are a mystery to everyone.

There are two theories in general circulation.

The first is said to be embraced by Claude Dupras, who ought to know, since he is a consulting engineer, and worked with Zappia on the plans for the village. That theory holds that Zappia, under extreme pressure from the Mounties, decided that he might be able to become a convention kingmaker, and thus gain enough influence to smooth things out. Pretty far-fetched, one might say. The other theory is even more so.

It holds that the RCMP, investigating Zappia's Olympic hanky-panky, found a large sum of unexplained money, which was in fact destined to be a contribution from construction folks to Mulroney, who everyone thought was going to make it, and therefore be dealing out contracts one day. The theory supposes that Zappia told the Mounties that the money was for the Tory leadership, and then, realizing what he had said and the consequences it might have, announced his candidacy to cover up.

We find it hard to subscribe to either theory, preferring rather to accept that anything to do with the Olympics is crazy and inexplicable, and leave it at that.

Whatever the reason for the Zappia effort, it is clear that he hired three Mulroney workers to get his nominating signatures. Some of them appear to have been forgeries, while others were bona fide signatures from people who thought they were signing for Mulroney again.

The three were fired from the Mulroney campaign after the episode. One of them was named Paul Delaney. A number of people, including several journalists and a member of Joe Clark's staff, were eager to persuade us that this was the Paul Delaney who was a crony of gangster Lucien Rivard and had several convictions for heroin smuggling. While Mulroney's Delaney may not have been acting in the best of faith, we are happy to attest that he is not the heroin smuggler. The discrepancy in age approaches forty years.

The RCMP is now investigating Zappia's nomination papers.

By the second day of the convention, Mulroney had spent $407,000 of other people's money. The total bill is estimated at $430,000 — rather less than the $750,000 estimated by many journalists, who having inflated The Candidate, felt obliged to inflate his expenses when they turned on him.

One wealthy Tory observed that "Mulroney spends money with all the insouciance of a man who doesn't have any." And he wasn't spending it effectively. For less than a third the price Joe Clark had a winning campaign run by professional amateurs. Mulroney had a losing campaign run by amateur professionals.

One room of the Mulroney house in Westmount has its walls covered from floor to ceiling with photographs of Mulroney with everyone even remotely well-known that he's met. Most of them are unrecognizable to anyone who hasn't made a lifetime study of insignificant ministers in long-gone Union Nationale cabinets.

You can take the boy out of Baie-Comeau, but you can't take Baie-Comeau out of the boy.

Dalton Camp

Saturday

The Sound of One Hand Clapping

"Why Hellyer?" we ask the man with the Hellyer button on his coat.

We are riding out to the arena to hear the candidates' speeches in a packed school bus rented for the convention, and find ourselves jammed into the back seat.

"It's personal I suppose. We had a meeting a couple of years ago; John Diefenbaker was supposed to speak but he had to cancel at the last minute. Paul was the only one who would come down to Newfoundland to speak to us. We became casual friends. Everytime I would come up to Ottawa we would get together for lunch."

"Doesn't Moores going to Mulroney influence you?"

"Not a bit."

"Why do you think Moores endorsed Mulroney?"

"He had to. Power Corporation is talking of building a big oil storage depot on Bell Island. And Christ we need everything we can get — since the mine closed there's absolutely nothing there."

There it is again. If Paul Desmarais and Power Corp. have indeed financed Brian Mulroney's campaign, even if they have made all the wild spending possible, they have also hung around his neck like an albatross.

"Well, what would Hellyer do for you?" we asked.

"I have a feeling that Hellyer has learned a lot in the past few years. If nothing else he knows how difficult it is to even get a plane from here to Newfoundland. Air Canada's charter reads that it must serve all Canada, but they've pretty well cut us off. And you can say that we also believe that Paul Hellyer as Prime Minister will give Newfoundland the same interest rates on loans that this man Trudeau gives to the Russians and Cubans."

"Wouldn't Mulroney do the same?"

"He has to get into Parliament first."

"So does Hellyer."

"We have a riding open — St. John's West. It's pretty well a safe seat, even for Mulroney, but he really has to win a seat in Quebec."

"Mulroney has already said that in the next general election he would run in his home town," we say.

"Good for him, and if he wins tomorrow he can keep our seat warm until the general election. We'd be glad to have him around even if it was just for a year or two." He says it without much conviction.

The bus reaches the arena and we pile out.

Unlike the first two days, even the upper galleries of the arena are almost filled, and the complexion of the floor and lower stands is quite different from what it has been. The crowd is more clearly segregated behind the candidates. Behind the stronger candidates the crowd is overflowing, squeezing in upon the weaker ones. Fraser's group has been almost pushed out the door. Gillies is being encroached upon, Grafftey is surrounded.

The Wagner section is packed, and his styrofoam bowlers — or battle helmets, depending on one's bias — are everywhere. Wagner's people have spilled out over the stands and occupy a good section of the floor.

The Wagner buses have arrived. That is the big news of the day. Picking the delegates up at staging points in Hull, they have brought them across the border in time for the 4 pm registration deadline. Registration official John Hayes, noting that only 15 to 20 Quebec delegates are still unaccounted for, tells the Montreal *Sunday Express* that "most of the missing links came in by busloads in the morning and afternoon, and I noticed about 80 per cent of them seemed to be Wagner supporters."

Wagner organizers dismiss the unkind suggestion that the delegates have been brought in late to avoid exposing them to the disturbing influence of other campaigns, saying that most of them are working people who couldn't get time off work, or afford the expense of a five-day convention. There's good reason to believe that the Wagner campaign is short of ready cash, and could only afford the rooms it is providing in Hull motels for two days — five would have broken the bank.

The group behind Jack Horner is impressive, especially for a candidate who has been written off so early.

"God-dammit," says a Horner floor worker, "Jack's looking stronger than we ever thought."

"Where are they coming from," we ask.

"All over."

"Seriously."

He points to Hellyer's section. "There are a lot of people who'll come to Jack on the second ballot if we are strong enough on the first. Maybe some will even come before."

"That isn't the way it seems to figure."

"Excuse me," he says dismissing us, "I've got these seats to fill."

John Fraser is to speak first. Just before he goes up to bat, we spot John Lynch-Staunton, a key Mulroney strategist, with a big smile on his face. He's rubbing his hands with glee over the plum position his boy has drawn in the speaking order — third, following Heward Grafftey.

(Lynch-Staunton's previous experience as a political strategist consists of losing the only two election campaigns he's ever fought. He became a Montreal City Councillor in the days when Mayor Jean Drapeau's Civic Party didn't need, or bother, to campaign. In 1968 he ran for the Union Nationale in a provincial byelection, losing to Liberal candidate Bill Tetley. By 1974, he was Drapeau's number-two-man on the city's Executive Committee, drawing a total salary of more than $40,000. In that year's municipal election the formation of an opposition coalition, the Montreal Citizens Movement (MCM), forced the Civic Party out onto the campaign trail, and Lynch-Staunton lost his seat in Côte-des-Neiges district to MCM candidate Nick Auf der Maur.)

Lynch-Staunton is taking time off from his new $40,000-a-year job as a financial consultant to BAREM, a Quebec agency that is developing a policy for high-speed regional public transport, to help out his old friend Brian.

Now Fraser strides grimly to the stage, accompanied by an honour guard of what look like superannuated flight attendants. It is a sad climax to a sad and underfinanced campaign.

American-style political conventions are relatively new to Canada, and we clearly haven't got the hang of them. For example, if they are going to continue the voting methods will have to change so that the actual voting doesn't drag out as long and there is more time to wheel and deal, to cross and double-cross. Perhaps delegations will have to caucus and vote openly as they do in the States.

Another weak point of our conventions is hoopla. Canada as a country wears its paper stickers and waves its banners sullenly and self-consciously. The once impregnable walls of Lutheranism, Calvinism and Jansenism that kept us secure in our inhibitions are badly battered, but this aspect of our psyche is virtually unchanged.

As the successive candidates are introduced to make their speeches, the hoopla ranges from the merely inane to the absolutely disastrous.

Fraser's unhappy entrance sets the tone for the day. Mulroney comes in with a crass brass band. The otherwise intelligent campaign of Joe Clark allows the candidate to be brought into the arena riding in a landau. Clark compounds the gaucheness with an opening line in which he apologizes to Premier William Davis for not wearing seatbelts — this is a joke, but not even Clark smiles.

And so it goes. Jack Horner has a tin band which plays the Triumphal March from Aida badly. Paul Hellyer brings in an expanded version of the fiddlers and stepdancers he has used throughout the convention with such little success. The only problem now is that as they spread out through the floor of the arena, nobody can hear them and few can see what they are doing. With his impeccable timing, Hellyer waits to one side of the stage until the music nobody can hear is over, thus giving the impression to the gallery that he doesn't want to speak. Sinclair Stevens must have bussed in the whole population of York-Simcoe but still manages to look merely silly.

Only Flora MacDonald's managers seem to realize that if this stuff has to be done, it is best to do it with some class.

She upstages everyone with an enormous pipe band playing 'The Skye Boat Song' in which an earlier MacDonald rows Bonnie Prince Charlie into exile.

The band is good, and it wins a response from the crowd. In the context of what comes before and after, it works.

But on the whole hoopla at Canadian political conventions is dealt a body blow this day in Ottawa from which, it is hoped, it will never recover.

More seriously, perhaps, the art of political rhetoric also passes another milestone in its decline.

Subtly, almost imperceptibly, the convention has taken shape and the lines have been drawn. The majority of delegates seem to have made up their minds, at least as far as their first-ballot votes are concerned. Other delegates, while still wavering between the personalities of two or three candidates, have also settled at least on the political direction of their votes.

Regardless of what the candidates will state, deny and disclaim in their speeches, they are, in the minds of the majority of the delegates, set in three moulds. Horner, Hellyer, Wagner and Stevens are on the right, Mulroney, MacDonald and Clark are on the left, and the also-rans are Fraser, Gillies, Grafftey and Nowlan — not to mention Quittenton. But with the exception of Dr. Q, even the last group is not in a wholly undesirable position in the twenty-four hours preceding the first ballot. They can be kingmakers, or more likely spoilers. They can also be an attractive refuge as a first-ballot choice while delegates wait for the power to show.

After the first ballot, things aren't nearly as simple. If any of the front-runners demonstrate real power on the first ballot, many delegates will rush to the winning side. Mulroney is counting on his bandwagon's flattening all objections to his leadership. And Wagner, with his 400 Quebec votes now present and accounted for, also feels he has a momentum that cannot be stopped.

But if neither Wagner nor Mulroney has the power to sweep all before him in the early balloting, a strong showing on the first ballot for Hellyer or Horner on one side and MacDonald or Clark on the other may allow one of them to replace the leader on his or her side of the party and then go into the finals.

The divisions have been clarified and the final ballot will be between the two major factions of the party — the winners and the losers. But who will represent each side on that last ballot is by no means determined, and will be decided by a whole complex of factors. So even if the number of first-ballot votes that will be changed by the speeches is relatively few, the impression that each candidate, even the spoilers, makes this afternoon is important, and for eleven separate reasons.

John Fraser suffers for speaking too early what Jim Gillies and Sinc Stevens are to suffer for speaking too late — nobody is listening. As he has throughout the campaign, Fraser sinks to the occasion. He speaks of politics as war, and promises to wage it. He also speaks of the lonely call of geese, and urges everyone to meet the challenge that awaits us.

(In 1973 the CBC television program *Up Canada* introduced a satire on Ottawa politics that was supposed to run for several episodes. The satire featured the adventures of the MP for Nookie and the Islands, George Fraser. The newly-elected MP for Vancouver South, John Fraser, was convinced that the program was directed at him and lodged a strong protest with the Corporation. The writers of the skit, who had never heard of

John Fraser and had just used as colourless a Canadian name as
they could think of, were somewhat amused. The CBC, however,
was not, and cancelled the satire after one episode.)

As Heward Grafftey gets into his speech, the smile on John
Lynch-Staunton's face disappears. Heward gives a rip-snorting
performance to roars of approval from all sections of the crowd.
He waves his arms about, pounds on the lectern, and says it all
— John A., John George, Robert Lorne, Trudeau and his
"monolithic uniform monolith," and finally, Party Unity. He
gets his greatest hand when he denounces the CBC for having
"packaged" Trudeau and engineered his election. The crowd
goes delirious, some shaking fists at the CBC booth, a kind of
plastic bubble suspended over one corner of the floor. John Bassett, who's doing commentaries for the rival to his own CFTO,
waves back and takes a bow.

Conventional wisdom says that you can judge a candidate's
standing by the amount of applause he gets from outside his
group of partisans. Grafftey's own group is the second smallest,
but he gets cheers and ovations from all over. Part of the cheering comes from sympathy, and from the fact that everyone can
safely applaud Heward, since he's no threat to anyone.

For a moment though, the applause given Grafftey is reminiscent of the same ovation given Joe Greene at the last Liberal
leadership convention. Greene, running perhaps to save his cabinet seat, played Abe Lincoln to a crowd of appreciative Liberals.
The speech got him enough votes to stay on for an extra ballot,
helping to stall a developing stop-Trudeau movement. And
Greene not only stayed in the cabinet, but got a promotion.
Remembering this, some observers figure that the number of
votes Heward can expect has risen from around thirty to perhaps
close to a hundred.

After the Grafftey fireworks, Mulroney is pure anti-climax.
The with-it, tough labour lawyer turned brash and scrappy politician delivers a speech with all the zest and punch of a birthday
card. The speech is not noticeably worse than that of most of the
other candidates, but outside his own section the crowd sits on its
hands. It is a remarkable and, in the circumstances, highly significant response.

During the introduction of Mulroney by Frank Moores and at
one or two points during the speech itself, Heward Grafftey
organizes a bit of a diversion.

He moves from his box to shake hands with Claude Wagner;
a cluster of Wagner supporters send up a cheer. Moores breaks
stride in mid-sentence. "Has Grafftey already thrown in with

Wagner?" runs the murmur in the crowd, and delegates are distracted from what is happening on the platform.

A little later, as Mulroney winds through his text — he is now clearly speaking to the western parts of the arena where his supporters are clustered — Grafftey does his little number again. This time he seems to be shaking hands with Flora MacDonald.

The Tory caucus has shown its dislike of Mulroney on several occasions. Although a joint letter opposing the candidacy of someone "without parliamentary experience" failed to materialize, most delegates here have received up to thirty-seven letters from individual MPs urging them, in effect, not to vote for Mulroney. Grafftey's little dance and handshake are another message to the delegates about The Candidate.

Mulroney's speech and its reception have merely forced his campaign to its inevitable crisis. Mulroney is the man around which all the frustrations and wrath of the party's losers have crystallized. There was no chance for him to conciliate and there was no chance that he could pacify the other side. People have come to this convention either to vote for him or against him. His only chance was to bull through the opposition, to create the momentum that would be unstoppable. This he has now clearly failed to do.

By the time Mulroney steps off the stage, it has already become part of the mythology of the convention that the speech blew it for him. The exchanges of "whaddya hear?" are transformed into "who wrote the speech?" Almost as quickly, a culprit is settled upon: it could only have been Peter C. Newman, the editor of *Maclean's*.

And that is no sooner rumoured than it is denied from all sides. Newman himself takes the trouble to deny it to us before we have even said it. In a letter dated February 26, he writes that "despite all the gossip that has been floating around, I did *not* have anything to do with Brian Mulroney's nominating speech," notes Mulroney's repeated denials of his involvement with the speech, and explains:

"I did go to Magog to interview him for a possible cover story if he won the convention. Six other journalists were at Magog during the same weekend on similar assignments, including Peter Desbarats of Global News; Ian MacDonald of the Gazette as well as representatives from CFCF in Montreal and Time magazine."

The denials are convincing.

However, there are still some curious circumstances surrounding the speech and the weekend meeting in Magog.

In the pre-convention issue of *Maclean's,* dated February 23, there is a piece headed "The Issue that Haunts the Tories." The issue is, of course, the Wagner trust fund. The article turns to the question of just how much Brian Mulroney knew about the trust. After hinting that he knew plenty, it goes on to say "Mulroney, in seclusion in the Eastern Townships just before the convention, was not available to respond."

What the article does not go on to say is that, as we now know, among the people with whom Mulroney was in seclusion was Peter C. Newman.

Others at the meeting at Magog that weekend included Mulroney's gnomelike campaign manager Michel Cogger, John Lynch-Staunton, and a representative selection of the Quebec Bar Association.

More interesting than the question of who wrote the speech is the commotion that has surrounded it. The speech itself, after all, is not the cause of Mulroney's defeat. It is no worse than, say, Joe Clark's speech, which will be good enough to win him the leadership. But it is the pin-prick that bursts the Mulroney balloon. He is now a leper. Peter Newman and everyone else are now mortally afraid of seeming to be even casually associated with the air of death that surrounds his campaign.

And so the authorship of the speech remains a mystery, and a classic one. Fifteen or so people in a secluded estate. One of them must have done it. The prime suspect issues a convincing denial.

We think the butler did it, if anyone still cares.

Curse You Red Tories

The second half of the dynamite sandwich that blows Mulroney out of the water is Pat Nowlan. He plays Jack Horner — in fact, as it turns out, he out-Horners Horner — lashing out in all directions at all the leading candidates: the apostasy of Paul Hellyer, the wild spending of Brian Mulroney and the false modesty of Flora MacDonald. He is also a bit too frank about the few obligatory words of French all the candidates have to throw in out of deference to the more than six hundred Quebec delegates. After interrupting his rabble-rousing to sputter a few French words about party unity and the like, he returns to English with "now let's get back to business."

Like Grafftey's, his speech is enthusiastically applauded, this time mostly from the Horner and Hellyer sections. And as with Grafftey, it is premature to read too much significance into the applause.

Next is Joe Clark, whose speech is at the same time the dullest and the most interesting of the afternoon. In an uncommonly bland manner — he is only now beginning to inch his body over the side of the trench — Clark forgets to describe Trudeau as the scourge of mankind and the Conservative march to power as a holy crusade. He does say that six more years of Liberal government will destroy the country, but in the context of this convention that is relatively mild stuff. The main message of his speech is simply that it is a good idea for the second party in the two-party system to get a bite of the apple once in a while. And unabashedly following up on Robert Stanfield's appeal of the evening before, Clark says that people are not interested in what the Conservatives are against but rather in what they are for. It is hardly a call to build a New Jerusalem but the tired and bored delegate, who has been treading all day in a sea of platitudes, is ready to grasp at straws.

Flora MacDonald makes her dignified entrance, and delivers a tightly-scripted speech that has a beginning, a middle, and an end, and is therefore judged one of the best of the day.

Earlier in the day, we ran into a Canadian University Press correspondent, who was wearing a Dr. Q button. Since the Quittenton campaign cost a total of $7,000, and his publicity brochure consists of an offprint from *Windsor This Month* magazine, which last summer ran an exclusive interview with Dr. Q in which he talked about his job as president of St. Clair College, we wondered where the button came from. It turned out to be one of those gold-and-black stick-on labels that come from hardware stores. Canadian University Press was also active in the night with letraset. But the supply of Q's was running low, and so one of us trudged off through the snow to the hardware store up the street to replenish it. As a result, as a delegate named Jim Kelleher mounts the podium to introduce Dr. Q, there is a small but noisy demonstration on the floor.

Kelleher gives an incredible rambling introduction about Dr. Q's accomplishments and the fitness of an experienced college president for the leadership of this great party. Finally, Dr. Q interrupts this lengthy encomium and launches into his speech. Delegates, observers and press recognize the signal for a coffee break.

As far as issues go, Dr. Q seems to be indistinguishable from the other candidates. The problem is the package.

He understands Quebec, he says, because "you don't sleep with a French Canadian woman, as I have for thirty years, without getting some messages." In fact, Dr. Q speaks better French than any other non-Quebec candidate. He doesn't bring up the wood-alcohol issue.

Dick Bonnycastle, the genius behind Harlequin Romances, introduces Jack Horner, And Horner adopts a tone more suited to the hero of one of the Milquetoast novels Harlequin publishes than to the mean, gun-toting cowboy his followers expect him to be:

> There is a band of hope that stretches across our nation — strong as steel — as broad as our land itself — as deep as the ocean that washes our shores, it is imbedded in our hearts — linking us together — uniting our strength and clarifying our vision.
>
> As I travelled our land from St. John's to Victoria — meeting you — listening to you — in our large cities — in our smaller towns — in our rural communities — I sensed this hope and I felt your concern.
>
> The message is clear and unmistakable.
>
> Our time has come.
>
> What is this band of hope that unites us — it is this — *we have had enough of divided dreams.*
>
> From the Grand Banks to the Gaspé — from Montreal to Medicine Hat — from Oshawa to the Okanagan — *we do not have divided dreams.*
>
> We all yearn for the same things.

Thick as it is, it is an effective speech. It is short and conciliatory, and it helps make Horner respectable. But it stuns his supporters. Waiting for Jack to cut the fluff and start using his knees in the clinch, they are momentarily silent as he walks away from the lectern, several minutes short of his time limit.

Next is another tough guy, Claude Wagner, and he too plays statesman. He picks up a lot of points with a smooth, reasonable speech. He holds out a future of law and order to a people "thirsting for justice and security." He reminds us of how grateful the Queen was for the fine protection she got during her visit to Quebec City in October 1964, when he was the provincial solicitor-general. As in his campaign brochures, this reference is made only in English, since many Quebecers have bitter memories of *Le samedi de la matraque* and Wagner's part in it.

He blames Trudeau for any bad feeling between French and English Canadians, and says it's now up to the Tories to heal such feelings. He says all the right things about Sir John A. and the rest, echoes Dief on unhyphenated Canadians, and walks off the stage leaving the impression of an honest, upright, dignified statesman, with real leadership qualities — a Quebecer with sense. The trust fund and the other ugliness that has surrounded Wagner's career are suddenly forgotten.

Next comes the last of the front-runners, Paul Hellyer. And all of a sudden the conciliatory note that has been struck by the last two speakers is abandoned. He launches an attack on the Red Tories, looking toward Flora MacDonald as he speaks, although the substance of his criticism applies to most of the members of the Tory caucus.

He sat in the House, he says, waiting for the Conservative party to measure up to his standards. It took a long time for this man, self-cast in the Churchill mould, changing parties to fit his principles and not his principles to fit a party, to throw his lot in reluctantly with the Tories. An obvious implication of his speech is that if he is going to lead the party a new standard of purity will be required.

It is not a formula for success. Boos and catcalls arise from pockets of the crowd. The rest of what Hellyer says is lost on many of the delegates. "I know what the people of Canada are looking for," he intones at one point, "and it isn't Pierre Trudeau." "It isn't you either!" bellows a man in the front wearing a yellow Clark scarf.

"I blew it," is Hellyer's judgment of his own performance as he steps down from the stage.

As with Mulroney, it is questionable whether Hellyer would have had a chance of winning whatever he said in his speech. The speech has merely brought the weaknesses of his campaign to a head.

Up until Friday night, Hellyer planned to use a prepared text, but then, remembering the disaster that had befallen him at the 1968 Grit convention, he scrapped the text and went to notes written on index cards. He and a campaign worker, Jack MacDonald, toiled over the cards well into the night. Early Saturday morning, MacDonald went over the speech with another member of the Hellyer campaign entourage, Dr. Jimmy Johnston. The speech ended with, "A hundred years ago, the Fathers of Confederation had a dream. Twenty years ago, John Diefenbaker had a dream. I too have a dream!" There was nothing in it about Red Tories. "All we need now," said Dr. Johnston, "is to find the keys to 24 Sussex."

But between then and the time he got up to speak, Paul Hellyer, all by himself, decided to change it.

His strategy — to draw the line sharp and clear and stake out his turf on the side that encompassed the most territory — is not an unreasonable one. The message he wants to convey to the delegates, which is that the Conservative party is worth supporting only if it is clearly different from the Liberals, is not extraordinary, at least from the vantage point of the Tory losers. And even the way he says it, in the context of a campaign and convention where attacks on Red Toryism have been a continuing theme, is not extreme. It is his timing that is all wrong.

For Hellyer has underestimated one crucially important element in the thinking of the delegates. Given the divisions within the party, people are looking not only for the leader of their choice, but also for the one who stands the best chance of being acceptable to the other side. The delegates who boo Hellyer were never going to vote for him anyway, but in announcing that he is the best leader for half the party, he has blown it with his own supporters as well.

The mood of the convention has become to find the leader who, by hook, crook or consensus, can make the party a credible alternative to Trudeau. And Hellyer has simply disqualified himself.

It's Crying Time Again

After Hellyer's performance, the speeches are effectively over. Delegates have been listening for almost four hours now and they have had more than their fill. Neither Stevens nor Gillies can arouse any interest. Even Sinc's appeal to vote for him as "the cuddly Conservative" doesn't get much response.

Afterward, Brian, Mila and the Youth for Mulroney have invited us all next door to the Coliseum for pizza. We accept, and mingle with the thin crowd, looking for delegates. Finding even fewer than the night before, we head downtown to do a final round of the hospitality suites and check out the two main bashes of the evening, a Wagner Pizza Party and a Clark Hoedown in adjacent ballrooms of the Château.

In the Château we find delegates by the busload, and they are taking the lobby by storm.

A sixty-piece young Kiwanis band, Les Eclairs, is belting out the tune we have already heard a little too much of — 'Alouette' — drowning out a second Wagner band, a small accordion group playing 'Auprès de ma Blonde' (another musical blunder, since that is the tune of Joe Clark's French song). Hundreds of supporters wearing white styrofoam bowler hats are stomping around and around the lobby chanting "Wagner! Wagner! Wagner!" Some have torn part of the brim off their hats, turning them into facsimiles of construction hard-hats; others have torn off the whole brim, so that what is left, inadvertently perhaps, resembles a storm trooper's helmet; one delegate has taken a bite out of his.

Wagner arrives, and the chant turns to a bellowing war cry. We take refuge from the crowd in the nearest tranquil place — the Mulroney hospitality suite off the lobby. Its only occupants are six elderly Wagner ladies from Montreal's East End, watching the Toronto-Buffalo hockey game on the giant Mulroney TV screen.

By 10 pm the convention is completely unglued. All the pre-game rituals have been observed and the delegates can now enjoy their last moments of being wined and courted. The atmosphere in the lobbies, corridors and ballrooms of the hotels is that of the night before Grey Cup. It is whoopie time.

Nobody gives a damn any more about the leaflets, brochures and policy papers. Any notion of who should win has been completely replaced by who is going to win and how.

By the elevators on the third floor of the Château lies a T-shirt. "Youth for Mulroney" is stencilled on the front. Somebody swoops around the corner, drink in hand, grabs the shirt and stuffs it into his pocket.

"Christ," he says, "are they already discarding these things?"

In John Fraser's suite there remains but a ravished platter of cheese sandwiches. One of us visits the can. Piped-in music isn't a surprise, but suddenly voices break in:

"You're gonna have a long time to think about what you've done, Joe. Murder one, two counts."

It seems that the Fraser organization has the Muzak speaker in the can connected to the TV, and it's playing *Hawaii Five-O*.

Between suites, one of us slips in to check out the bar, and falls into conversation with an uncommitted delegate couple from Merritt, B.C. They tell us how their riding association ran an Indian as the PC candidate in the '75 provincial election. All thirteen chiefs in the region supported the candidate, and promised to deliver the entire Indian vote — 35 per cent of the riding. They didn't. And, says the couple, that's what it's going to be like tomorrow—the Chiefs won't be delivering the votes of the braves.

In Flora's suite, we meet three of the six delegates from Prince Albert, Diefenbaker's constituency. They tell us they're sticking with Flora all the way, and they think they can persuade the other three, too. If not, the other three are probably going with Joe Clark.

Wagner's rooms are pretty quiet, but the action is somewhere else. Wagner is due to visit his pizza party downstairs at any time and that will be the signal for the crowds to materialize — Wagner's is the real moveable feast. When his entourage sweeps through the hotel, the crowds follow.

There is a smell of defeat at Paul Hellyer's bash, compounded by an appearance by Paul himself with a statement which seems to apologize for his attack on the Red Tories this afternoon. By morning most delegates will be given a letter which appears to retract the retraction. Although not yet running out of mouths, Hellyer is definitely running out of feet to put in them.

In Joe Clark's suite, the Man Himself is present, taking a breather from the hoedown downstairs. He is confronted by an earnest young delegate and is trying to explain his ideas of decentralization of key federal social services. He does a good job and visions of "community control" and "power to the people" dance in the kid's head. But he wants more details, and Clark, now being gently shoved from the room by one of his handlers, politely puts his questioner off. But the kid is clearly impressed.

There are a lot of young delegates at this convention. The PCs have a constitutional provision that of the six delegates from each federal constituency, two must be under the age of thirty. In addition, there are delegates representing party clubs organized at universities and colleges.

In late summer when we interviewed one of the members of the party's office staff, we were told that there was a bit of a rush to organize and charter campus clubs. There had been fewer than fifty organized clubs before the leadership convention was called. Now they were sprouting up all over the place. As we spoke with Mike McCafferty he was repeatedly interrupted by long-distance calls. Each call required a patient explanation of the proper procedure for becoming officially recognized.

"What do you mean, you haven't elected any officers, just convention delegates . . . No that's all wrong. You have to do it by the rules."

Next call: "Look, he's the sitting member down there, you can't go behind his back . . . Well, I don't know, call another meeting, invite him to speak and get somebody . . . now this is very important . . . get somebody to take minutes."

"Everybody's anxious to get organized and get elected as delegates," he told us, "before the crunch comes and the challenges begin."

We suggested that there appeared to be a lot of loopholes in the rules for voting delegates, which could become important if the leadership race became close. Yes, he agreed that there were, and that the safeguards the national office had developed were pretty easy to evade:

"A request for a charter has to be signed by twenty-five registered students. We can check with the registrar, but if they just copy the names from the student directory, there's no way we can really check. All the registrar can do is confirm that so-and-so is a student."

"Is there any evidence so far that this spate of organizing is being done on behalf of any one potential candidate?" we asked.

"We have our suspicions, and we're keeping our eyes on the situation. But it's really too early to tell."

At the convention, the youth vote seems to be as divided as any other group. If any candidate was successful in the early manoeuvrings to organize student clubs, it is not apparent now.

Before Clark can make his exit from the suite, two men move in to block the exit. "Joe, I'd like you to have a few words with one of our fisherman friends from Nova Scotia."

The other man moves forward and shakes hands with the candidate. "I have a few questions about the 200-mile limit."

Clark's handlers are getting impatient. "There are a few people you gotta meet tonight. . . . they've been waiting now . . ."

"A 200-mile limit isn't going to save the industry back east," says the fisherman, moving between Clark and his handlers. "The real problem is conservation. . . . I'm in no trouble yet, but it's coming."

"Well of course it's a complicated problem, and I'm no expert. The enforcing of a limit must be a first step to protect our resources."

"Maybe we can discuss it later."

Clark picks up on that to break off the discussion: "We should keep in touch."

Clark is gone now. The fisherman, his friend and the earlier questioner form a group in the room.

"Joe has this one quality; if he doesn't know, he'll tell you he doesn't know — and he'll listen."

The fisherman is non-committal, the kid nods in mild agreement and the group disperses.

As it turns out, the fisherman is actually a lobsterman and claims he isn't suffering a bit yet. "They call us the Cadillac fishermen," he says. But in terms of capital investment he figures he is not doing well at all, and the real problem is the future. "In a few years there will be nothing left of the east-coast fishery. I've done all right. Christ, after the war I never dreamed I would get where I have. But there's nothing for my kids."

We ask him what he thinks of Joe Clark's chances.

"He's won already. . . . He won't get it tomorrow, but he has come from nowhere, and he'll be a force in the party. That's for sure."

Standing against one wall is Trevor Jones, one of Sinclair Stevens' campaign workers. Jones has been in the room for some time, mostly chatting it up with some of Clark's workers.

One of us says, "I think Stevens would be a good finance minister in Joe Clark's government."

"I do too," says Trevor Jones, smiling.

Joe Clark's presence at the convention is as it has been throughout the campaign. He is unobtrusive but he is always around.

His campaign seemed adequately financed — apart from Alberta money, of which he had plenty, Clark also had some Bay Street support, notably from the McCutcheon family of Canadian General Insurance, Acres Ltd. and Guaranty Trust. (The family's patriarch, the late Sen. Wallace McCutcheon, was an unsucessful Tory leadership candidate in 1967.)

Nevertheless, Clark was not in the Mulroney league as a spender. But the money he did have was carefully and wisely spent.

There were few signs of Clark groupies greeting delegates at the airport or station and there were no Clark buses transporting them. But we were told that Clark got the jump on the other candidates by having his material distributed to the delegates as the they left for the convention instead of when they arrived.

Clark's printed material was substantial, and serviceable in the sense that there was always some fresh stuff at his tables. But his stuff had nothing of the flash — or the expense — of Horner, Mulroney, Gillies, or Stevens material. Tories don't appear to be big readers anyway.

Clark had his hospitality suites in the major hotels as did everyone else, but, except for two occasions, he kept a low social profile at the convention. Wednesday night there was a low-key affair in his suite at the Château and tonight there is a more elaborate hoedown, still modest by convention standards, in one of the smaller Château ballrooms. There were no Eat Grits Breakfasts with Joe Clark, nor did he serve Alberta beef and British Columbia salmon at luncheon.

But Clark always started early, and seemed to get the biggest bang for the buck. And tonight is no exception. Waiting in the near-deserted Wagner party for some pizza to appear we can hear the music of the country and western band coming from Joe Clark's hoedown.

As we come in the band is playing, "I got my first guitar when I was fourteen, now I'm over thirty and I still wear jeans." The room is crowded and the vibes, as they were Wednesday night, are good. Joe and Maureen bounce in, and a few words are said: "C'est un great plaisir for Maureen and moi . . ."

Clark's fluent bilingualism (which the media have upgraded from the "moderate bilingualism" a New Brunswick paper credited him with early in the campaign) is so fluent that he frequently uses both languages in the course of a single sentence. As many French-speaking observers have put it, "Il se débrouille" — he gets by. He can't dance either.

In the Clark gathering, the Wagner one — which comes alive with the arrival of the pizza and the candidate — and the corridor in between, options and permutations for the next day are the only topic of conversation. The dealing between the candidates that is going on all the while must be getting difficult. One's chief rival on the first ballot may well be one's ally on subsequent ones. Flora MacDonald's main rival is now Joe Clark, yet when things get testy tomorrow they will have to link arms. The same applies to the other side. Wagner must overcome Hellyer, or vice versa — and what of Horner, Gillies, Stevens, Nowlan and even Grafftey? All kinds of pressures must be applied, but the persuasion must be gentle. Another problem: who can speak for whom? While the strategists are upstairs, the voting delegates are downstairs, slapping backs and drinking up a storm. They have their first-ballot choices made, and most know the direction they will go on subsequent ones.

By the process of elimination, Joe Clark has become a front runner. But the big question mark is Flora MacDonald. If she runs ahead of Clark on the first ballot, the momentum will swing to Wagner on the other side. Mulroney has a lot of first-ballot votes, and nowhere to go but down — many Clark and MacDonald voters do not like him. The spoiler candidates seem likely to drift to Wagner. But who can tell?

We meet Claude Wagner's Thunder Bay organizer. He thinks it will be his man against either Clark or MacDonald on the last ballot. And he hopes it's Flora — for two reasons. One is that he is kind of partial to Clark himself and "I wouldn't have to make the choice between him and Wagner on the last ballot." And he also isn't sure his man can beat Clark in a straight showdown.

"But if it's Flora we'll win. Most of these people just won't vote for a woman."

"And they will vote for a French Canadian?" we ask.

"Well," he says, "we may win by ninety-four to eighty-six."

The television coverage of the convention today seems to have brought a lot of people down to the hotels. We speak to a middle-aged couple, who couldn't resist getting in on some of the action and excitement. They are life-long Liberals, but as the man keeps repeating, "We're just fed up with the drift." He won't, or can't, get any more precise. His wife points to a Joe Clark sign: "We like him."

Would they vote for him?

The man shrugs. "We've always been Liberal, you know."

The pay-for-your-booze rule, although badly bent at times, has more or less stood up — the hotels have made a killing. And now that it is just about over, it's time to try and cash in some leftover booze tickets. This is not as easy as it seems. Each hotel has its own. A handful of Skyline tickets gets nothing but sympathy from a bartender in the Château.

Last call for the bar.

In the line at the bar in Clark's hoedown we meet The Manitoba Youth Director For James Gillies. As events suggest, this title is longer on description than substance. He has in tow a member of the executive of the Manitoba Young Progressive Conservatives, and behind them both stand a gaggle of YPCs.

"Where do you go after Gillies?"

"We still like Jim."

"Yes, but where do you go after Gillies is out?"

He takes a Clark button from his pocket. "But it's not as simple as that," he cautions. "I made up my mind to support Gillies because of all the candidates, I agreed with what he said most. Whether he can win or not isn't, at least wasn't, so important. But now it comes down to what's best for the party."

"But isn't Gillies most likely to support Hellyer or Horner?" (Wagner seemed out of the question, considering some of Gillies' campaign pronouncements.)

He shrugs and walks away.

To say that Jim Gillies' campaign never got off the ground would be to overestimate its impact. It never even made it to the runway.

Yet when Gillies was first elected to the House of Commons

in 1972, he was clearly a major addition to Tory ranks. Former Dean of Administrative Studies at York University and Chairman of the Ontario Economic Council, his academic credentials were respectable enough that he was named to be one of the Tories' triumvirate of finance critics, along with Stanfield and Marcel (Porky) Lambert, an inoffensive Edmonton lawyer and former speaker of the House.

Why Gillies, whose economic knowledge far surpassed that of Lambert and Stanfield, was not named sole finance critic is something of a mystery. According to Dr. Jimmy Johnston, it was because he refused to kowtow to Dalton Camp. Nevertheless it was Camp who, as late as December, raised the possibility of a Gillies victory in the leadership campaign. This would have occurred on the sixth or seventh ballot; as delegates' first, second and third choices dropped off, Gillies, who is disliked by relatively few in the party, would look better and better. Gillies would have had to get more than eighty-seven votes on the first ballot, however, to make that possible.

Gillies' political career almost began back in the early sixties, when he taught at the University of California at Los Angeles; in 1962, he was approached by members of the campaign committee for Richard Nixon, who was running for governor of California against Pat Brown, and asked to write speeches. According to Gillies he "never did anything about it," but a newspaper biographical sketch later described him as having "worked for . . . Richard M. Nixon in 1962."

He spent fourteen years at UCLA before coming to York, and much of his style and philosophy comes from his American experience; there is still a trace of California in his speech. Among the ideas he picked up from the United States was wage and price controls, which he began to advocate in 1973 and disowned after they were adopted by the party.

It was also in the United States that Gillies began his business career, which he pursued on his return to Canada. He picked up a scattering of directorships, including one with Fidinam (Ontario) Ltd., establishing for that Swiss-based development company a Tory connection of the sort that can be valuable in Ontario. In 1971 the provincial cabinet approved a property deal between Fidinam and the Workmen's Compensation Board. A month later Fidinam donated $50,000 to the Ontario Conservative Party. Gillies by this time had taken a leave of absence from the Fidinam board, and he formally resigned from it on February 1, 1972, on his appointment to the Ontario Economic Council. Later the story of the Fidinam deal got out and became one of the scandals that weakened the Davis government. Gillies, ruminating on the affair afterwards, said, "I almost wish I hadn't resigned from the board before so that I could have resigned then." But in September 1972 Fidinam was still using Gillies' name as a member of its board.

Another company on whose board Gillies sat was a small but fast-growing investment concern called the St. Maurice Capital Corporation (later Commerce Capital Corporation), which has been the business vehicle for some of the more highly-placed members of the Liberal party-civil service set, including Sen. Jack Austin, Maurice Strong of PetroCan, Bill Teron of CMHC, and Paul Martin, Jr., son of the former External Affairs Minister.

His political campaigns have always been generously infused with money, and in 1972 he took on one of the freest-spending Liberals in the country, Bob Kaplan (who had spent $68,000 to defeat the luckless Dalton Camp in 1968) and not only outpolled him but also outspent him. In the leadership campaign he outspent all of the other candidates except for Mulroney.

Gillies launched his campaign with a speech in early September in which he attacked the performance of the Conservative party over the last few years and the direction the party was taking, or rather the lack of it. It was an attempt to clear himself of what was supposed to be the chief rap against him, which was that he lacked "toughness" and "bite". It started people asking whether perhaps what he really lacked was political judgment. During the campaign he skated skilfully down the middle of the ideological split, he attracted some Bay Street support, and his performances always got good press notices. But he never got through to the delegates; even Dr. Johnston, his old college roommate and longtime friend, found himself unable to support him. If there hadn't been so many candidates, and if they hadn't all rushed so furiously toward the centre where he started out, Camp's scenario might have worked for Gillies. As it was, the scenario panned out, as Mulroney's scenario panned out, for Joe Clark.

We begin to think that, despite all the criticism of American-style political conventions, they do at least make some people think about the political process. And the analogy between this evening and Grey Cup eve is maybe rather superficial: this isn't completely a spectator sport. Nobody gets a vote at the Grey Cup game.

They're playing the last dance at Clark's Hoedown:

> It's crying time again,
> You're going to leave me,
> I can see the faraway look in your eyes. . . .

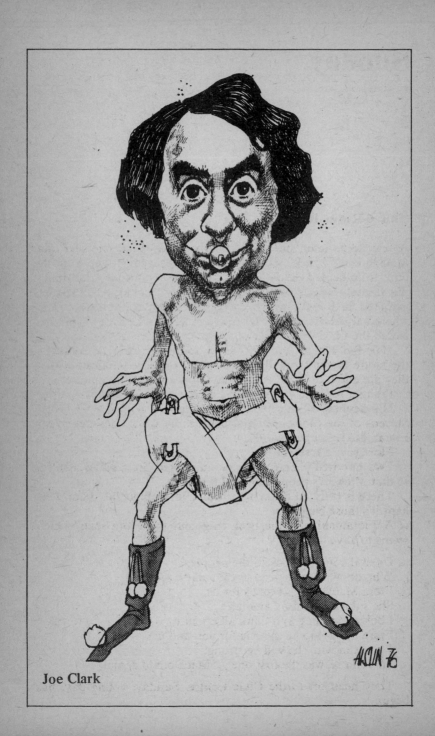

Joe Clark

Sunday

Sinc decides to buy

A few hours later, one of us finally makes it to one of Flora MacDonald's breakfasts, by the wily stratagem of sneaking up on it from behind. Eddie Goodman opens the meeting, introducing himself to a crowd of more than a thousand Floraphiles gathered in the Adam Room of the Château, the same room where only hours before the strains of 'It's crying time again' had closed the Clark Hoedown.

"Hi, I'm Knute Rockne," says Goodman. And he could be the Notre Dame football coach, except that the implication that they are about to Win One for the Gipper is a bit premature.

Premier Richard Hatfield says more than a few words.

His nephew Michael Hatfield, hailed as a genius by Geoff Stevens of the *Globe and Mail* because he is Mr. Computers for Flora, also says a few words.

Flora says a few words.

Two hundred people get huge numbered breastplates affixed, so that Michael's people can find them.

There is truly an air of Death or Glory about the room. Perhaps it's those bagpipes.

A Floramaniac at the back rings out the Flora song, which seems to have no tune:

Open the nation, look to the people,
Who do we want to lead us on and on and on?
Flora MacDonald, Flora's for us,
She's the leader for Canada!
Look all around you, think all about it,
Flora has got to be the one for you and me!
Flora can win, she will be strong,
Sir John A. was the first one — MacDonald again!

They head off to the Civic Centre. Sunday, voting day, has begun.

At the Civic Centre, delegates who not only had the time but in fact seemed eager to discuss the merits and chances of any number of the leadership candidates when we spoke to them a day or two ago now have neither time nor inclination to talk to anybody except other voting delegates. Everybody has found a place to sit and sign to wave. Many have even found places in the organizations of various candidates.

"Can't talk to you now boys — got some people to see."

And so it goes. The crowd streams into the arena, laden with snow, wet and disgusted with the weather. And they are going to be there for hours and hours, jammed into the bleachers, with only the induced excitement of the occasion to sustain them while the relentless lights turn the area into a steambath.

The information booths of the candidates are now command posts for the war of the signs. The television sets, which until this morning were playing video cassettes, are now tuned to one of the networks. In the long hiatus between ballots, these television sets will become points of congestion as delegates cluster about them hoping to find out what is going on.

In the stands, Wagner hats and signs clearly dominate. There are plenty of Mulroney signs as well. In the upper reaches of the northwest corner of the arena there is a Mulroney sign on every seat. There is nobody sitting there however.

Overall, the scene in the arena emphasizes the importance of the outcome of the early fight between Mulroney and Wagner for the Quebec delegation. If the fight over delegates in Quebec had been even close Mulroney could have come to this convention with enough challenges to wound Wagner mortally, but he was so outgunned in Quebec, he couldn't even do that. Had the impressive support Mulroney was able to gather in other parts of the country been buttressed by support of the Quebec machine, he would have been in a position to win. But now, as we look down on the sea of Wagner signs, the what-might-have-beens no longer matter. What does matter is the tremendous edge the machine vote from Quebec has given Wagner.

As the voting begins, several hours late, it looks as though Claude Wagner may have it all wrapped up.

For the observer, the action on voting day — the announcements of the ballot results — occupies a total of perhaps ten minutes, spread over eight hours. And the convention floor is now off-limits to most of the press (our one floor pass has gone to our photographer) and we are confined to the remote ends of the arena, the mezzanines and the top galleries. The best way to pass the long stretches waiting for the ballots to be completed is to watch one of the television sets in the back of the press room, and in fact print reporters do most of their coverage sitting in front of the Teevee. Still, one gets restless there, and periodically goes to do another tour of the arena to overhear what's being said on the walkie-talkies, which is usually what was being said on the TV half an hour ago. One of us lost his press pass in last night's festivities and, after being told in no uncertain terms that a replacement is impossible for security reasons, borrows one from a nineteen-year-old female student (which seems to be quite acceptable to the Tory security men) to get in on the inaction. Later we find out that the missing press pass was turned in and given away to somebody else.

Meanwhile the counting of the first ballot drags on and on.

There's evidently a refugee from the sixties with a bad case of brain bubbles co-ordinating the musical efforts throughout this convention. Only a truly wasted saboteur could have programmed the Muzak for the long first ballot wait with such favourites as 'I'm a yankee-doodle-dandy', 'Yesterday' and 'Those were the days'. A saboteur with a knowledge of Tory history. Dalton Camp, perhaps.

The floor is overrun with Wagner organizers screaming into walkie-talkies. In a quiet corner, both members of the Grafftey team are standing about a yard apart, also screaming into walkie-talkies.

"Can you hear me? Over!"

"What? Over!"

With the first ballot still unannounced, well over an hour late, we have the leisure to reflect upon the distinguished career of Michel Côté. As chief legal counsel to the City of Montreal — and therefore the power behind Montreal's Finest — he dreamed up such brilliant measures as: the bylaw forbidding mingling in bars, which was declared *ultra vires* and canned; the bylaw forbidding newspaper boxes on Montreal streets, which was declared *ultra vires* and canned; and the bylaw forbidding astrologers in Montreal, which was declared *ultra vires* and canned.

He was also the chief negotiator for most major Olympic contracts, which it is hoped will be declared *ultra vires* and canned. And his father was the only minister ever to be kicked out of Maurice Duplessis's cabinet for corruption.

At this convention, Michel Côté is chairman of the Elections Committee, which is responsible for organizing the counting of the ballots.

Any organizational foul-up notwithstanding, there are a number of problems built into the voting system. Delegates are registered by number and assigned according to that number to the different polling stations. Each delegate passes along a table where his name is checked off by a clerk and he is given a ballot. At the end of the table is the booth where the ballot is marked and put into the ballot box. After a given amount of time the polls close and the clerks and scrutineers decamp for a sealed counting room where the security is so tight that even the convention chairman can't enter to try to hurry up the counting. The room has even been de-bugged.

The random assignment of delegates and the tight security in the counting room are presumably designed to thwart any attempt to telegraph the vote before the official announcement. It is all one of those complicated arrangements that seemed like a good idea at the time.

Meanwhile all candidates are doing their best to circumvent the system, because it is of vital importance to them to know as early as possible how the votes stacked up. For one of the by-products of this long and complex voting procedure is that there is little time between ballots for candidates to do their deals.

When it finally comes to the crunch, all the spotters and floor men, all the computer feed-outs are relatively useless. The candidates, in the main, depend upon counting the number of badges the voters wear as they troop through the polling stations. These unofficial counts that the candidates receive through their spies are wildly inaccurate.

This, however, doesn't stop the CBC "election desk" from virtually declaring Claude Wagner elected a good hour before the first ballot is counted — on the basis of an unofficial count leaked by a Wagner official.

The first ballot gives Wagner a lead — 531 votes to 357 for Mulroney, who is second — but nowhere near the 650 votes that he needed to make him unstoppable. Horner, with 235 votes, has shown unexpectedly well and will be a factor in what follows; Hellyer, with four votes fewer than Horner, is finished. On the other side, Mulroney has no possibility of increasing his total by very much, and so any stop-Wagner movement will now focus on Joe Clark, in third place with 277 votes, 63 ahead of Flora MacDonald.

If this leadership campaign and convention were run on more classical lines, this would be the moment for the spoilers or king-makers. If Gillies, Stevens, and Hellyer had control of their delegates they would be forces to contend with, and perhaps they

could even steer the convention to Horner. Unlikely as this outcome appears, Horner has run a strong campaign at this convention, and he is certainly in tune with the gut feelings of a lot of
the delegates. Many good, solid Tories simply distrust Wagner,
and Horner could be their best option.

We remember a conversation we had with a delegate who was
ideologically in tune with Stevens, and therefore could be
expected to follow along the line to wherever it lead — to Hellyer, Horner: but the man balked at Wagner. "When he spoke at
one of our meetings, he was evasive about the trust fund. As if
he didn't want to look us in the eye. I just can't vote for a man
like that."

But there is no chance to find our man now and find out what
he is going to do.

Grafftey, as the candidate with the lowest total (Dr. Q with-
drew before the balloting, throwing the weight of his delegate to
Wagner), is eliminated. When his vote total, thirty-three, is
announced, a cheer goes up from the whole convention. More
sympathy.

He moves beside Joe Clark. Jim Gillies, with eighty-seven
votes, withdraws and does the same.

Paul Hellyer waits by the phone for Stevens to call, for Horner to call, for anybody to call. He looks as if he doesn't know
what has hit him.

Now the question is: what will Sinc Stevens do? His 182 votes
have placed him out of contention, and he withdraws and begins
his walk across the floor, pursued by microphones and cameras.
The CBC announces that he is going to Joe Clark. Then it
announces that he is going to Paul Hellyer. Then it announces
that he is going to Claude Wagner.

The CBC reporters who found out that Stevens had deals with
Hellyer and Wagner were, of course, not wrong. But now
Stevens tells the microphones and cameras that he is supporting
Joe Clark. The Wagner people, who smell victory but know they
need help, are furious; the Hellyer people, aware that they've
reached the end of the road, find themselves unable to get too
angry (except in extreme circumstances it is difficult to get too
angry at Sinc Stevens for anything, because whatever he does he
seems to be having such a good time doing it).

Hellyer quits waiting by the phone and moves to Wagner. But
it is too late: the voting has begun and he is on the second ballot.
John Fraser also withdraws and goes to Clark; he too is still on
the ballot.

Stevens, in the mythology of the convention, becomes the
kingmaker; it will later be widely believed that he had victory to

give and gave it to Clark. But while helpful to Clark and a major morale-booster for his forces, Stevens' move is not crucial because the majority of his votes were going Clark's way in any case. Far from controlling his delegates Stevens was, in effect, controlled by them. He went to Clark because he thought Clark was going to win. As one observer puts it, "Sinc sized him up as if he were a penny mining stock and decided to buy."

During the lull of the second ballot, Party President Michael Meighen comes out with a shock announcement. In this very country, in this very Civic Centre, brought all the way from England at enormous expense, is Sir Frederick Bennett, a member of that time-honoured club, the real House of Commons, come for the first time in history to observe a Canadian leadership convention, joining hands across the water between like and like of different nations, to the greater good of World Conservatism. Mesdames et Messieurs. . . .

Unfortunately, Sir Frederick, unaware of two nations, two cultures, B & B and the rest, figuring he's been sufficiently introduced, seizes the microphone before the French-speaking delegates have a chance to hear about the renaissance of World Conservatism, and launches into his speech.

In England, he says, we do things a little differently. Not to say there's anything wrong with all this, but it is, really, well, honestly, a little confusing. Real Conservative Party leaders, in the real Conservative Party, are chosen only by members of the House of Commons. And the word 'Progressive' in the party name. There's nothing really wrong with that either, but. . . .

Nobody is paying much attention.

There is plenty of movement on the floor. Microphones are thrust in to almost every passerby's mouth — everybody has something to say and it is all very important.

Behind the stands there is also a great deal of activity. Moving through the congestion around the television sets are very purposeful-looking Wagner men dragging boxes of signs to sections where MacDonald and Mulroney delegates sit. From the opposite end, Clark signs are being infiltrated into the arena.

With five candidates already out of the race, many people are now voting their second and third choices. The impression made by the nice young man from Alberta who is everybody's second or third choice is beginning to pay dividends.

There are some Mulroney supporters who can't be convinced. One of us asks a well tanned and tailored man with about four Mulroney scarves around his neck what he will be doing if Mulroney drops. "Whaddya mean. . . . it's Clark that has to

come to Mulroney. Can't you read the vote? Brian is second; he
has almost a hundred votes over Clark. In fact, I just heard that
after this vote Clark will give the handshake to Brian. And there
is no way in the world for Flora to vote for Wagner."

Apprehension and distaste in the National Capital Region

The second ballot is announced. Clark has passed Mulroney.
Much more important, Wagner's momentum has been slowed.
He has 667, to Clark's 532. Nowlan, with 42 votes, MacDonald
with 239, and Horner with 286 are all equally dead. So is
Mulroney, with 419, but he will stay on for one more ballot. His
supporters seem curiously unconcerned. They know they have
lost, but they still wave their signs. Meanwhile Clark signs are
pushed at them. Most don't reject them, but lean them to one
side for later use.

Behind the stands a small group is furiously working on old
Hellyer and Horner signs. They are tearing off the old posters
and replacing them with Wagner ones.

In Clark's section, the air is electric. Flora MacDonald walks
over to shake hands with Clark, while the Albertan's organizers
move into Flora's section. Somebody has thoughtfully left a
stack of Clark signs at the exit nearest Flora's seats.

Flora's progress toward Clark, slow, regal and firm, sad yet
proud, to the victor the vanquished, is attended by a minor riot
of electronic journalists, falling over each other and the entourage, trying desperately to find out where she's going.

"Flora!" shouts CBC, "Flora, are you going to Joe Clark?"
There's no reply.

"Flora!" he shouts, "Flora! I don't know how long my microphone cable is . . . and Flora seems to be heading toward Joe
Clark, and I'll pass you back to Lloyd Robertson."

Flora's first words on achieving the promised land, delivering
on her promise, are "j'ai venue." I have come. Except that verbs
of motion take 'je suis', not 'j'ai'. The Tories' solution to the
French Canadian problem seems to be to *bilingue* them into
submission.

While both TV networks are still trying to rustle up a few delegates who are prepared to testify to the undying hatred between
the English and the French, Pat Nowlan is making his way
across the floor to the Horner Ranch. The two vigilantes say little more than "Howdy, pardner" before it's out into the dust

once more, to do what a man has to do — in this case, to add
their combined might to the defenders of the free world in the
Wagner camp.

Horner takes time out on the way over to stomp on a persis-
tent radio reporter, which action is lauded by all right-minded
people, especially those from the print media, who've had more
than enough of being trampled by a horde of spotty upstarts
with microphones and cameras. But, this doesn't stop a pile of
people from rushing into print to analyse the depth of Horner's
hatred for journals and journalists.

About ten minutes later, as the third-ballot lull settles on the
arena, we decide to go looking for Dr. Q for a post-defeat interview. By mumbling "looking for Doctor Quittenton," a way is
made through the Wagner benches to where he had last been
spotted. One of us is wearing a tape-recorder, with the microphone attached to the shoulder strap, partly for taking instant
notes, and partly as a passport in a world dominated by people
wearing such things. The machine is running, ready for Dr. Q,
when the neighbouring face seems awfully familiar. It's Stompin'
Jack.

Nobody's noticed the tape recorder, which is half picking up a
hurried conference between Horner and a key aide. Nobody,
that is, except sundry members of the Horner family.

Jack's brother Hugh, the deputy premier of Alberta, a dwarf
John Wayne, threatens violence, but it's nothing that can't be
dealt with. Brother Norval looms up. Again, no problem. Sister
Mrs. McCorkel, who is built like a brick outhouse on square
wheels, joins in, towering with rage about what sneaks like us
have done to Brother Jack's chances to lead this Great Party.
That's it — we retreat.

We get another insight into Horner's mediaphobia a little later, listening to the tape. There is no doubt that his family and
partisans are genuinely angry at the press, but what about Stompin' Jack himself? What is being said in his whispered conference with a key aide at a tense moment?

"Jack, the people from *Canada AM* want to know if you still
want to go on in the morning."

"Sure, they'll have to come to me. Tell them to send a car to
the hotel before eight."

He turns to another helper and says, "You know, I reckon we
ran a pretty good show, so long as we come out financially."

This is the man who's boiling mad at the press and everyone
else.

(He did go on CTV's *Canada AM,* and put up another fine show, ranting that he would never send his grandsons to fight for a free press.)

The results of the third ballot are announced: Clark 969, Mulroney 369, Wagner 1003.

The Wagner bandwagon has been stopped. It is estimated that two thirds of the Mulroney votes will go to Clark, which will give him victory by a clear if not comfortable margin.

In the Mulroney section both Clark and Wagner workers are handing out signs, but the Clark signs seem to go at a rate of about three for every Wagner sign that is snapped up. In the Clark section everyone is waiting for Mulroney to come over, and the anticipation turns to disappointment as the realization filters through the section that Mulroney isn't moving. But the disappointment is tempered by the knowledge that his delegates are going to Clark anyway, and many Clark supporters figure that the reason for Mulroney's reticence is that he is afraid that an open display of support for Clark might tilt the convention to Wagner.

Dalton Camp is in the press room, looking pleased as punch. But he is still acting coy. His non-committal grin stretches from ear to ear. "You can never tell in these conventions though," he says to a few people standing around. "It's getting late, and people are leaving — it just takes a hundred or so to decide to go home, and things could change."

But people don't seem to be leaving.

A Montreal CBC reporter who bet heavily on Mulroney is walking around the press room with a wad of bills, handing them out to everyone in sight.

It is still possible to find people who are predicting a Wagner victory. Some argue that Mulroney's Quebec delegates will go to Wagner because in the end blood will tell. Others suggest that they will vote for Wagner because they want to get safely home to Montreal tonight.

But in fact, kinship, geography and language play no part in the final division into winners and losers. Sixteen of the nineteen MP's from Alberta are now supporting Wagner.

In the arena itself there is a stark difference in mood between the Clark section on the west and the Wagner group on the east. Among the rank-and-file delegates who have followed Hellyer and Horner to Wagner, there is plain discomfort. Hellyer has already gone home, and Jack Horner and Claude Wagner make a very awkward couple. The people wearing Wagner hats are grim and determined. Those wearing Horner boaters are just grim.

There is more noise and shouting and a sense of excitement in the west end of the arena: the melding of groups there seems more natural. But generally, as the crowd waits for the final vote, things are rather quiet.

The final vote is announced.

"Clark 1187."

A cheer grows from his end of the arena, but it seems to be a bit uncertain. A rather large man with a Wagner hat on his head stamps his foot. "No . . . no . . . that's not enough, not enough..."

"Wagner 1122."

There is a cold murderous silence in one half of the arena and much cheering and commotion in the other. The feeling in the Clark section is as much relief as elation.

Wagner delegates begin streaming from the floor. This movement to the exit stops briefly as Wagner reaches the stage to make his speech. There is no trace of the shock and rage that were written on his face the last time he lost a leadership convention, in Quebec City in 1970.

At that convention for the Quebec provincial Liberal leadership, Gisèle, sitting beside him, was the first to react when the result was announced.

"Claude!" she shrilled. "On s'en va!" She stood up, grabbed him by the arm and started to leave.

Pierre Elliott Trudeau, aware that this would probably happen, had taken steps to prevent it. Sitting next to Wagner was old friend Bryce Mackasey, who held the federal seat in Wagner's riding, Verdun. His instructions were to get Wagner up on the stage, for the sake of party unity, at whatever cost.

Mackasey grabbed Wagner's other arm, and pulled.

For several minutes the tug-of-war continued.

"Claude, let's go!"

"Claude, come on, don't be silly, you know you have to go up there. . ."

"Claude! We're going!"

Gisèle lost the battle by a hair and Mackasey stiff-armed Wagner up onto the stage to accept his defeat.

On the stage are all the defeated candidates except Hellyer. They all seem to be making the best of an uncomfortable situation, except for Jack Horner who stands impassive and unapplauding. He will leave the stage before Wagner is introduced.

Wagner's speech acknowledging defeat, and calling on delegates to make the election of Clark unanimous, is even more masterly than his Saturday speech.

Columnists are rushing to their dictionaries for synonyms for noble, statesmanlike, diplomatic, gracious, moderate, magnificent, generous. Again the circumstances under which Wagner came to the Conservative party and the other less than savoury aspects of his career are forgotten.

As Robert Stanfield begins talking, the delegates in what was the Wagner section of the arena again begin streaming toward the exits.

John Diefenbaker is nowhere in sight.

To the half of the arena that is listening, Joe Clark gives his acceptance speech, which like Wagner's is more or less a repeat of his Saturday performance. He says that "we will not take this country by stealth or storm but by hard work."

Even the Clark section is getting restless now. Finally the party on stage breaks up.

Claude Wagner steps down and leaves by the back way.

Taking time off from electronic punditry, Bryce Mackasey is moving in the opposite direction.

They shake hands.

"That was a close one, Claude. But I see they didn't have to pull you up on the stage this time."

They both laugh.

An hour or so ago, between the third and fourth ballots, a curious announcement came over the P.A. system in the press room: Brian Mulroney would hold a press conference after the final result was announced. Now, overcome with curiosity about what he could possibly have to say at this point, we go to the same dank room in the back of the Civic Centre where the Alberta cabinet ministers reaffirmed their support of Joe Clark on Friday night.

There are about a half-dozen reporters there, the ragtag end of the press corps, all of them looking as drained as we are. There is no sign of Brian Mulroney. We sit around for ten minutes or so and post-mortem the results, having lost the ability to talk about anything else. Finally a Mulroney aide shows up.

"The press conference is cancelled."

Epilogue

Blue Grit from High River

Brian Mulroney did have a press conference, albeit an informal one, surrounded by a knot of reporters on the floor of an almost-deserted Civic Centre, near the northeast exit. He did not have much to say, but he did suggest that there had been a gang-up (or, as Charlotte Gobeil said on the TV, "gangbang") of the other candidates against him.

An hour or so later the CBC local newscast led off with a five-minute in-depth report on the weather, and then continued through a fire, the heart attack suffered by Tom Cossitt, the MP for Leeds, at the convention, and non-competitive sports in Ottawa schools. Ottawa had returned to normal.

Except for a third-floor walk-up warehouse in the Glebe, well off the beaten Ottawa track. There were cots and hamburger wrappers from four nights of striving still littering the floor. There was another country and western band, but Christine refused to give just one more chorus of 'Old Joe Clark.'

Beer, wine and the occasional bottle of harder stuff flowed, although not quite so copiously as the Pernod and orange juice at a Jean-Yves Lortie party. The whole thing had the flavour of those rare NDP victory parties in school basements, and it occurred to us that perhaps out west NDP victory parties would be even rarer in future.

The Clark Quebec delegation organized a pretty good party, too. It was still going full swing at about 3 am when we arrived at the Inn of the Provinces. An elderly lady from Abitibi summed up the general mood: "C'est un tabarnak de bon party."

In the basement of the Beacon Arms Hotel, Brian Mulroney's wake had the air of a victory party, which seemed a little curious under the circumstances.

Disappointed supporters were told, "Don't worry, this was a victory for us. You'll have a chance to work for Brian again."

Brian sang the last song of his campaign, 'My Wild Irish Rose', and issued thanks all round.

It is clear that Brian Mulroney thinks he has a political future. The question is where.

One of the more imaginative scenarios proposed is that Mulroney's back-up position all along was that if he didn't win the leadership, at least he could become the first Tory premier of Quebec.

Mulroney consciously copies the late Daniel Johnson, even down to matters of speaking style. He can come off as a Québécois to the francophones and, unlike Johnson, as an English Quebecer to the anglophones.

He may well think that he can unite the province's young conservative nationalist federalist forces with the old conservative federalist nationalist forces, pick up the entire English vote, disenchanted Liberals, and those who vote Parti Québécois as a protest against Bourassa rather than for separatism.

He probably also has in the back of his mind that the first Tory premier of Quebec would be a lead-pipe cinch for the next national leadership convention.

He might even be able to overcome his most glaring disadvantage in comparison with Bourassa: he changes his shirt only five times a day, to Bourassa's six.

We tried this scenario out on a veteran observer of the Quebec political scene. "Hogwash," he said, "René Lévesque and the Parti Québécois are going to win the next election and invite Mulroney to be the Vice-President of independent Quebec."

He meant it.

On Monday, Opposition Leader Clark did not go to the House, but Claude Wagner was applauded from all sides when he entered. The highlight of the day's question period was the performance of a Tory member, Stan Korchinski, who was extremely agitated at the failure of the automobile manufacturers to produce small, energy-saving cars and ignored the Speaker's repeated instructions of "Order" until he was finally calmed down and restored to his seat by an avuncular George Hees. Clark ceremonially moved into the Centre Block office of the Leader of the Opposition for the benefit of the television cameras; he laughed when a reporter showed him a Toronto *Star* headline that said "JOE WHO?" and again when another reporter called him "Mr. Sharp." The press, which had all but ignored him throughout the campaign, was now blaming him for being unknown.

Global TV ran the documentary it had been preparing on Brian Mulroney, noting at the beginning that even though he didn't win, he might have.

On Wednesday Clark took his seat opposite the Prime Minister for the first time. He was ushered in with a round of welcoming speeches, including a particularly apt one from Trudeau, who took his text from a letter he had received from Michael Meighen saying that "never has the need for an alternative to Trudeau and his party been more apparent" and asking him to contribute (tax-deductibly) to the Conservative party. Clark's reply was by comparison a bit forced; picking up on a remark by Ed Broadbent, he said that the NDP leader's "problems of internal disunity may continue; ours of course are over." Then the preliminary bows were over, and the duel began. Clark, gracious if a little awkward a moment ago, was now combative:

"Here we go. Mr. Speaker, I would like to direct my question to the Prime Minister. What cuts in spending is the government going to announce to cut its deficit of five billion dollars?"

"For the first time since Trudeau has been in office," said one observer, "he has a real opposition. And he will rise to the occasion."

There was wide agreement outside the Conservative party, if not inside it, that the Tories had made their best possible choice. The NDP was becoming worried about the ability of a Clark-led Conservative party to cut into their support. "Quite inadvertently," said one senior New Democrat, "and in a total rejection of its past history, the Conservative party has acted in its own best interests."

One of the few dissenters was a reporter who argued that the Tories would have done better to choose Wagner. Trudeau had come to power, he said, because English Canada wanted to vote for a French Canadian who would keep his fellow French Canadians in line. Trudeau had blown that with bilingualism, 'French Power' and the rest, but Wagner, who with his speech on Saturday had established himself as a credit to his race, might be able to re-establish that original Trudeau constituency. On the other hand Clark, who was really no more bilingual than Stanfield, could not expect to make significant gains in Quebec, while in Alberta there was a danger of Horner's bolting the party and cutting into the Tories' western support.

It is not an entirely implausible argument. But it makes the same mistake that reporters made from the beginning of the campaign: it underestimates Joe Clark as a politician.

If the complex of factors that led to Joe Clark's victory can be reduced to a single reason, it is that his political skill was superior to that of any of the other candidates. He had a surer sense than the others of what the delegates wanted to hear and what they wanted the new leader to be, and he moved more quickly than the others to accommodate those wishes.

Joe Clark is, above all else, a professional politician. He lists his profession as 'journalist' but his forays into journalism have been brief and halfhearted. His reach for the top in politics has been steady and singleminded.

According to his own account, his mother was one of three known Liberals in High River, Alta., while his father, the publisher of the High River *Times*, was a lifelong Tory. In 1957 he was swept up in the Diefenbaker fever that ran through the country and the west in particular; he was one of the many who thought that maybe, just maybe, this man might make things change. The conflicting family influences were settled in his mind, and he went on to become a Tory *apparatchik*: private secretary to Alberta Conservative leader Cam Kirby, and then national president of the Progressive Conservative student federation for two terms.

Like two of his fellow candidates for the leadership, Flora MacDonald and Brian Mulroney, he came to politics from the inside, and it is no coincidence that these three were the candidates furthest from the party's loser psychology. Like MacDonald and Mulroney, he recognized in the mid-sixties that John Diefenbaker had to go. Ultimately, success for a professional politician is measured in elections won and seats gained, and by 1966 Diefenbaker stood in the way of those goals.

This is not to suggest that Clark does not have ideas or principles. He does, but they were obscured during the leadership campaign for two reasons. One is that they were consistently ignored or misunderstood by the press, and the other is that Clark himself is flexible about them.

Clark, along with MacDonald, has been called a Red Tory, but it is a misnomer. The term was originally used to describe philosophical conservatives who have a socialist strain in their ideology and ally themselves with socialists in the face of the common enemy: liberalism, and especially Yankee liberalism. Harry Stevens, the refugee from R. B. Bennett's cabinet whose Royal Commission on Price Spreads exposed some of the horrors of Depression Canada, was a Red Tory; George Grant, the author of *Lament For A Nation,* is a Red Tory. But there is no

socialism in Joe Clark's philosophy, and little traditional Toryism. He and MacDonald are really small-l liberals who happened to find themselves in the Conservative party — what
might be called Blue Grits.

His ideas differ from those of Pierre Trudeau in detail: in
important detail, but in detail nevertheless. Blue Grits tend to
have less faith in the federal government and more in provincial
and local governments than true Grits, perhaps because the Conservative party does not control the federal government but does
control several provincial ones. They also are more optimistic
that small business can be preserved in the face of growing mon-
opolization, and a more human form of capitalism restored, than
are Liberals, who despite their tinkering with competition policy
have an abiding belief that bigger is better.

In this support of the independent entrepreneur, the Conservatives are acting as spokesmen for one of the most faithful ele-
ments of their constituency, the small businessmen who have
been among the chief losers in the economic changes that the
country has undergone since World War II.

Clark has also placed considerable emphasis on the value of
encouraging the survival of smaller communities and argues that
urbanization and the depletion of small towns, while partly the
result of social forces beyond the control of any government, are
also encouraged by federal policies, for instance a passenger
transport policy that builds up air transport, which serves only
large cities, at the expense of rail transport, which can serve
small towns as well.

In the case of some of the more innovative programs of the
Trudeau government, such as Opportunities for Youth, Local
Initiatives and the extensions of Unemployment Insurance,
Clark thinks not that they are wrong in principle but that they
have been wrongly administered, and would like to see local
governments have a greater say in their administration. He suggests that if there is a specific problem — for instance, seasonal
unemployment among fishermen in Newfoundland — the
federal government should deal with it through a specific program, and not through extensions of an existing universal program that might be unnecessary elsewhere in the country.

These ideas are not particularly more progressive or more
reactionary than those of the Liberals. They are, however, interesting, and in many cases might be worth a try.

Whether Joe Clark as Prime Minister would try them is
another question.

Many of the nuances in his positions and much of the origi-
nality in his thinking tended to get lost as the leadership campaign went on. If at the beginning Clark's alternatives to universal social programs were specific measures to help Newfoundland fishermen, by the end they also included means tests for
family allowances.

Clark's initial statement on foreign affairs was, in effect, an
endorsement of the Trudeau government's policy of encouraging
relations in diverse areas of the world to counterbalance Canada's traditional ties with the United States. "The Third World
countries," he said, "are developing new power, which will force
the more developed nations, including Canada, to turn aid
towards the development of the infrastructure of Third World
countries. One harsh reality is that, as these nations develop,
they will begin to compete with us economically. We have no
practical alternative but to anticipate the dislocations in our
economy and, where necessary, adjust, rather than risk the rup-
tures of violent conflict between rich and poor." But at the convention Clark delivered every bit as ringing a defence of the
United States as Jack Horner, and threatened withdrawal from
the United Nations if the Third World countries didn't shape up.
By the end of the campaign he even had nice things to say about
the idea of a private-enterprise post office.

He was of course responding to the right-wing sentiment in
his party, and it was precisely because he responded so skilfully
that he is now Leader of the Opposition. But next on the agenda
for him is to become Prime Minister, and the perceptions, positions and prejudices to which he has to respond to do that are
rather different. For Canadians may get bitchy, selfish and into-
lerant but at bottom this is, as Brian Mulroney said, not a right-
wing country. The task for Joe Clark now is to bring his ideas
back into line with that wider political climate without losing the
allegiance of the losers in his own party. It is a task that has
defeated more than one of his predecessors in the Conservative
leadership.

At this convention, the winners gained a decisive victory over
the losers. The vote on the last ballot was in no sense reflective
of a left-right split within the party. The machine that Claude
Wagner has put together in Quebec can deal at least as easily
with Joe Clark as it could have with Jack Horner or Sinc
Stevens. As for the dissenters in English Canada, Horner and
Sean O'Sullivan and the rest, they have little choice but to go
along.

For they lost this convention fair and square. It was an open fight and there is little basis for a charge that the convention was machined. Even Dr. Jimmy Johnston, who squawked for nine years about Dalton Camp's manipulation of the 1967 convention, has few complaints about the 1976 one. "Democracy spoke," he wrote in the Cobourg *Star*. "The Tories have a potential Prime Minister, and hopefully a good one. There are a few political bruises. But it is the first Conservative meeting we have seen in years from which most of the people went home reasonably happy. The albatross of Dalton Camp's influence is dead."

With John Diefenbaker politically buried at the convention, and with Robert Stanfield in full support of the new leader, there is also little likelihood of the kind of party leadership-in-exile that has existed for the last nine years.

It is not so much that the losers have reconciled their differences with the winners as that they have accepted their defeat. But their deeper frustrations remain.

For the small businessmen and local entrepreneurs who form the party's base, the people whose expectations in life have been interfered with and are now ultimately threatened by the concentration of economic and social power in Canada, "big government" is the visible manifestation of the enemy.

This base has felt that control and direction of their party has been taken from their hands. The sour aftertaste of the defeat of John Diefenbaker has grown more bitter in the wake of the successive defeats the party has suffered under Stanfield.

And the speeches and actions of Pierre Trudeau over the past few months have fed the ideological paranoia of the average Tory. Things got so hot within the party during the later stages of the campaign that two obscure candidates, Heward Grafftey and Joe Clark, warned that the Conservative party could be walking into a trap set by Trudeau: a devious plot to place the Tories way out in right field.

Throughout the campaign the losers had the stage, and while most candidates protested that the only hope for the Tories was "up the great wide middle," the atmosphere was revivalist-fundamentalist, and eventually everyone was forced to the political right.

But the losers had two insurmountable problems: they did not have a credible spokesman and the Progressive Conservative Party of Canada is a very serious political party, which is not going to be taken over by a fringe.

The end result is that the Tories' electoral prospects are now arguably as promising as at any time since Trudeau became Prime Minister. Joe Clark is by no means a shoo-in for the next election, but a victory could well be within his reach.

And such an outcome would concentrate the mind party wonderfully.

A couple of weeks after the convention Mila Mulro gave birth to the baby that had been expected on The proud father said that they had been considering boy John George, but under the circumstances, they him Ben, after Brian's father.

Unlike her husband, Mila didn't peak too soon.